* * * * *

'A deeply validating reminder that peace *is* possible, however your brain works! It's super refreshing to find a book formatted in a way that caters to those of us who struggle with focus. Thank you for a book we can finally read without worrying we're "doing it wrong"!'
– **I Am Paying Attention,** the late diagnosed ADHD and Autistic community for badasses

'ADHD an A–Z is like having a friend walk you through your early journey with ADHD, when the NHS websites are full of scary symptomatic speak. Leanne's book is exceptionally well written, via the lens of an ADHD-er for ADHD-ers – the book packs the latest research from experts in the field of ADHD and personal lived experience, which gives readers a sense of validation and solidarity. What's most important is that the book is accessible, practical and broken down in manageable chunks – perfect for someone with ADHD.'
– **Samantha Hiew,** PhD, founder and director of ADHD Girls Ltd

'A fantastic user-friendly book which is both an excellent resource for those working with ADHD clients and also a bible for adults as they navigate their journey pre-diagnosis, validating their daily life experiences and giving them strategies to manage their ADHD and live their best lives.'
– **Dr Rob Baskin,** independent consultant adult psychiatrist, ADHD specialist

'A fantastic manual that does exactly what it says in the title: explores the key issues that are really pertinent to anyone with ADHD from A to Z. The book's format is really accessible for ADHD-ers – you can scan the contents and dip into the chapters that are most relevant to you. Each chapter is packed with really interesting ideas, lots of practical advice and exercises to complete, and it's all written in a really engaging way. An absolutely invaluable resource!'
– **Sonia Ali,** author of *A Teenage Girl's Guide to Living Well with ADHD*

* * * *

ADHD
an A–Z
Figuring it Out Step by Step

Leanne Maskell

Foreword by Ellie Middleton

Jessica Kingsley Publishers
London and Philadelphia

First published in Great Britain in 2023 by Jessica Kingsley Publishers
An imprint of Hodder & Stoughton Ltd
An Hachette UK Company

1

Disclaimer: The information contained in this book is not intended
to replace the services of trained medical professionals or to be a
substitute for medical advice. You are advised to consult a doctor
on any matters relating to your health, and in particular on any
matters that may require diagnosis or medical attention.

A CIP catalogue record for this title is available from the
British Library and the Library of Congress

ISBN 978 1 83997 385 7
eISBN 978 1 83997 386 4

Printed and bound in Great Britain by TJ Books Limited

Jessica Kingsley Publishers' policy is to use papers that are
natural, renewable and recyclable products and made from wood
grown in sustainable forests. The logging and manufacturing
processes are expected to conform to the environmental
regulations of the country of origin.

Jessica Kingsley Publishers
Carmelite House
50 Victoria Embankment
London EC4Y 0DZ

www.jkp.com

MIX
Paper from
responsible sources
FSC
www.fsc.org   FSC® C013056

Contents

This book is dedicated to everyone who has ever thought that there is 'something wrong with them', but who couldn't figure out what it was. Everyone who has been told that they're being 'dramatic', or that ADHD isn't real, or who has had to wait months or years to receive help. It is for the people who have felt so overwhelmed by the tsunami that is their own mind that they didn't know how they could go on any longer, but who have somehow kept fighting. For everyone who has felt like they're in an ocean that's filled with fish swimming one way, and you can only swim the other way. For all of the people who have felt like the 'odd one out', because they see the world differently.

I wrote this to provide an overview of my personal experiences in relation to ADHD, in the hope that it can help somebody else in a similar position. It's not here to convince you that you have ADHD, and I'm no medical or academic expert, just a person who has navigated this immensely difficult process and managed to finally live a (relatively) stable, happy life with ADHD. I've done my best to translate my own experiences and the overload of academic and non-academic information that exists into accessible, tangible and relatable action, straight from my ADHD brain to yours.

Thank you to everyone who has helped me along the way, including my family, who have always tried their best with what they had available to them at the time.

Foreword

I used to think that being smart meant being complicated. I thought that it was explaining complex concepts, using fancy words and speaking in long sentences. I thought it was the person at the front of the room who knew so much more than everyone else, *knew* that they knew so much more and gave you that little uncomfortable feeling in your stomach when you realised you'd never understand things in the same way they did. Recently, though, I realised it's actually the opposite.

Being smart isn't about being complicated. It's about taking something simple, but not yet obvious, and explaining it in a way that makes people go, 'Ahh, yes, of course! I knew that, I just hadn't seen it that way before – now that I have, that makes a huge amount of sense!'

This is exactly what Leanne has done in *ADHD an A–Z*.

Learning how to hack your ADHD – and how to work with your brain rather than against it – is absolutely life changing. But none of it is rocket science. It's a series of tiny changes, minute switches and small habits that all add together to make a huge amount of difference to your life.

It's learning to work in sprints instead of marathons. It's learning what external motivators you need to keep you accountable. It's understanding the way that your brain works and figuring out different ways to keep it happy. It's coming to terms with the fact that, actually, there is nothing wrong with being different – and it's much better to accept your differences and work *with* your brain than to keep your head in the sand and keep working against it. It's forgiving yourself for all those times you thought you were lazy, messy or unmotivated – and forgiving those around you who called you those things, too. It's deciding that you don't have to live in the way you've always been told you 'should'; you can instead decide to live in a way that feels more authentic to you.

Most importantly, though, it's realising that, yes, ADHD might have made some things trickier for you (and it might continue to make things tricky!), but it's also responsible for some of the amazing strengths, personality traits and quirks that make you *you*!

I was diagnosed with ADHD in October 2021 at the age of 24; since then, I've committed a huge amount of time to understanding my brain. I've spent time finding new ways of working and living, and I've worked on figuring out which parts of society feel authentic to me and which parts I'd just been forcing myself through without ever knowing that I'm wired to work differently.

I considered myself quite an expert on the subject and I thought I'd found a lot of the answers. But I still read through this book and found new perspectives on every page. I had an infinite number of those 'Ahh, yes, of course!' moments, and I finished each chapter with an array of post-it notes covered with ideas to implement, quotes to live by and things to consider. I felt refreshed, I felt ready for whatever challenges might come my way and I felt motivated to put some of the tips and tricks I'd learnt into practice. I felt more accepting of my 'Ferrari brain', I felt understood and I felt like I'd entered a new level of acceptance of and forgiveness for myself – like I'd shed another snakeskin layer of masking.

I was lucky enough to meet Leanne really early on in my ADHD journey. We met online after I'd started speaking up about my new diagnosis – I felt an instant connection and was relieved to find, for the first time in my life, someone who was *just like me*! We both have the busiest of brains, we both have huge ambitions, we both want to really make a difference and we both experience our days with a sprinkling of chaos. Since then, I've been super grateful to know Leanne as a friend, as an author and recently as an ADHD coach, too. But, no matter which hat she's wearing, the difference she has made to my life – in terms of happiness, belonging, productivity and acceptance – has been huge.

I am a happier person thanks to Leanne, and I am a million times more accepting of, and actually grateful for, my whizzy brain. I can't wait for you to feel the same happiness, acceptance and gratitude after reading this book. You deserve it.

Ellie Middleton, Autistic and ADHD advocate

Introduction

Throughout my life, I've felt like there's something wrong with me. As a child, I couldn't work out why other kids bullied me or how anybody else managed to concentrate in class. When my teacher asked the entire class if I'd cheated in my exams because I'd managed to get straight As, I wondered if I had somehow cheated simply by being myself.

I couldn't remember anything, but I could somehow cram it all into my brain before an exam. I felt lazy, stupid, and so chronically embarrassed by myself that I dived into any behaviours I could find that would help me stop overthinking, from binge-drinking alcohol to eating disorders. I couldn't imagine my future – I just felt lost. I remember crying on my 11th birthday, as I hoped to receive some sort of Hogwarts-style letter giving me a reason for my 'weirdness'.

This didn't go away when the future arrived. I'd picked to study law at university because it 'sounded good', and my friend went there. No matter how hard I tried, I could not listen in the lectures. I'd go in determined to concentrate, and leave feeling like the lecturer had spoken Chinese for an hour. I sat down to study my pages of reading, and always ended up doing something else, like going out clubbing. Even so,

I managed to graduate with a 2:1 by cramming it all into my brain at the last minute.

After graduating, I couldn't decide what to 'do' with my life, couldn't figure out how to get a job, and had missed all the deadlines and timeframes for graduate schemes that other students had applied for. Along with losing the structure of full-time education, I lost the limited control I had over my executive functioning. It felt like a nursery class had taken control of the classroom.

I spontaneously broke up with my partner of five years, moved out, stopped and started multiple jobs, had fights with all of my friends and family, and moved to Australia. I'd deliberately get as drunk as I could to manage my overwhelming anxiety from day to day, and the impulsive, bad decisions kept piling up on top of each other. Before long, I was in doctors' surgeries explaining that I believed I was going 'crazy'.

Some doctors said I was fine because I had a law degree. Others said I only maybe had 'emotional issues', and recommended therapy. One recommended a massage. Eventually, I learned that only an expert psychiatrist could diagnose me with a 'serious' mental health condition, which would cost hundreds of pounds. Before long, I was suicidal, trapped in a place of helplessness and powerlessness. Fortunately, I managed to survive long enough to see a private psychiatrist at the age of 25. I vividly remember going to see him, as just beforehand I was pacing around a park, trying to stop myself from spontaneously booking a flight to Mexico as the answer to my problems, before deciding that I could not live my life like this any longer.

I'd never suspected ADHD and didn't even see this as being

an option for what I was experiencing. However, being diagnosed finally felt like getting the Hogwarts-style letter I was waiting for – it was like being told I was a witch who had been living amongst Muggles for my entire life. There was a reason for my immense pain and loneliness, and I wasn't the only person in the world experiencing it.

It definitely wasn't an overnight solution to my problems, but it set me on the path of self-acceptance that I hadn't believed existed.

I went from seeing zero point to my life to publishing a best-selling book, *The Model Manifesto*, that was featured on the cover of *The Times*, and being a guest on *Lorraine*. My relationships with family and friends went from being dysfunctional to stable and secure. I stopped feeling like 'normal' jobs were off limits to me and worked in law for over two years.

The more I learned about ADHD, the more I understood, accepted and empowered myself, which enabled me draw on my experiences to do the same for others. I wrote this book, became an ADHD coach, and trained companies like Microsoft on neurodiversity. I continue to watch my life thrive beyond anything I could have possibly imagined only a few years ago, when I almost ended it all. Many people are not so fortunate – one in four women with ADHD have attempted suicide (University of Toronto, 2o2o).

I wrote this book to help other people navigate this path, because it can feel like you're walking through a thorny, tangled mess in the dark. It can feel lonely, demoralising, confusing and frustrating, especially with waiting lists for assessments of up to seven years long in the UK, and an overload of information online.

I hope this book will be the safe, clear hand you need to guide you on this path. Once you get through the thorns, I promise the view is magical. Understanding your own brain allows you to be compassionate, empathetic, confident and happy. There are many positive aspects to ADHD which mean, with the right environment, you can truly thrive with these unique cognitive benefits. Please hang in there and fight for the support you need.

How to read this book

I wrote this book in an A–Z format so that it can be picked up and dipped into. Each chapter discusses a different aspect of ADHD, so you can just pick what you want to focus on and go for it, with zero guilt about not 'finishing' the whole book – just reading the page is finishing it!

I also personally find it very helpful to write in my books, so please feel free to draw all over this one if you're reading the hard copy, underlining or highlighting things as you go. There are exercises in every chapter designed to help you understand your own brain and overcome any challenges you might be experiencing. Many of these are based on my experience as an ADHD coach, so it's kind of like self-coaching.

Please feel free to contact me at www.leannemaskell.com to discuss coaching, resources or anything else that I can help with.

is for ADHD

Did you know?

- ADHD is a neurodevelopmental condition that is associated with high levels of impulsivity, hyperactivity and inattention. Although there are different subtypes, ADHD is now generally used as the official recognised medical term (instead of Attention Deficit Disorder), regardless of whether a person has symptoms of hyperactivity.

- Children and adults can both be diagnosed with ADHD. In 1990, only 40 children in the UK were on medical treatment for ADHD, which means many adults have not been treated or managed properly (LancUK, 2016). Symptoms can appear differently at different ages.

- There are structural differences in the brain between those who have ADHD and those who do not (Cherney, 2019). Although there is no clear cause, it is said to be highly heritable, with a 75 per cent genetic contribution of ADHD (Vanbuskirk, 2018).

Attention Deficit Hyperactivity Disorder (ADHD) is a neurodevelopmental condition, which means that people who have it are neurodiverse. Our brains are wired differently to most people (referred to as 'neurotypical'). One in seven people have a neurodivergent condition, and 4 per cent of the global adult population have ADHD (Brody, 2015).

Although it can be very challenging to live in a world which caters for brains wired differently to mine, it's also not necessarily a bad thing. Just like Harry Potter thrived after learning how to use his brain, whilst still fundamentally staying in the same overall world, we can do the same – having ADHD is not a bad thing. It just means we're unique, but we have as much value and worth as anybody else.

A brilliant example I heard of this is thinking of the majority of the population as having a brain like the Microsoft Windows operating system, whereas ADHD-ers have brains wired like Apple MacBooks. Both programmes have their pros and cons, but, fundamentally, a Mac is not the same as a Windows computer. If a Windows user tried to put in their commands to a MacBook, they'd become very frustrated at it not 'working' in the way they're used to, and vice versa. No matter how hard we try, we're never going to able to change our operating software – and this isn't a bad thing! We just need to be able to understand what we're working with.

There are different types of ADHD, including the 'hyperactive and impulsive' type, the 'inattentive' type, or a combination of the two. The inattentive type is sometimes referred to as Attention Deficit Disorder (ADD), but ADHD is now the predominantly used medical term, as the subtypes are considered to fall under the same condition.

The inattentive type includes symptoms such as not paying attention to detail, making careless mistakes, failing to pay attention, not listening, being unable to understand instructions, being distracted, and forgetfulness. Women are more likely to be diagnosed as inattentive because they may be better at repressing their symptoms, as in 'X is for X-treme Differences in Women'. However, in my experience as an ADHD coach, the hyperactivity is nearly always mental rather than physical, with symptoms such as intense daydreaming or overthinking.

From a medical perspective, the hyperactive and impulsive type of ADHD has often been associated with physical displays. For example, fidgeting, squirming, getting up often when seated, moving around at inappropriate times, having trouble being quiet, talking too much or interrupting, and appearing as though they are 'on the go' or as if 'driven by a motor'. The combined type is a mixture of the above. Although neurotypical people may have similar experiences, the reason for the 'Disorder' part of ADHD is that these things happen to us to an extent that seriously impacts our lives. For example, anybody may lose their belongings from time to time, but not all of us have to spend a huge amount of money on replacing door locks or keys, laptops and mobile phones every couple of months!

Similarly, we might all struggle to focus at times and feel distracted, but not to the degree of simply being unable to do it at all. For example, I work with students for whom it takes six hours to write an essay, whereas it takes their fellow students a couple at most.

Some people are diagnosed as having a specific 'type' of ADHD, though others might not be. I wasn't. There is no one way that ADHD manifests in everybody, despite the image of a hyperactive child that your mind may have automatically conjured up. I was the dreamy girl in the back of the class, staring out of the window, completely unable to listen and quite often falling asleep. I hated P.E. but my knees often jiggled under the table. I was very quiet in social settings but my mind was constantly racing with thoughts.

However, there are common ADHD traits that might appear differently in different people who have ADHD (referred to in this book as ADHD-ers):

→ **Having a short attention span and being easily distracted:** This basically summarises ADHD in one line – an intense difficulty in concentrating. Our short attention spans means that we may have 'monkey brains', jumping between thoughts like a monkey hopping from one tree branch to another without stopping. My brain often feels like a television with 15 channels playing at the same time, and the remote is nowhere to be seen. It can make things like listening very difficult!

→ **Hyper-focus:** In sharp contrast to the above point, ADHD-ers may have an ability to hyper-focus on something that they are interested in, focusing so much that they stop thinking about other things that might be important. For example, working on a project for the entire day without eating any meals. This can cause frustration as we *can* pay attention if it is something we're truly interested in – but if not, then it is incredibly difficult to motivate ourselves.

→ **Carelessness and a lack of attention to detail:** Many ADHD-ers are 'big picture' thinkers. They may have brilliant ideas, but not be so great at executing them down to the minute details. I feel as though my brain works at a speed of 150 per cent, which means that I can forgo details in the rush of thinking fast.

→ **Being unable to stick to tasks that are tedious or time-consuming:** ADHD-ers might be very quick to say 'yes' to things, without checking the details – for example, thinking about whether they *actually* want to do something, the difficult bits included. We tend to not deal so well with repetitive administrative tasks and are on a constant search for novel and exciting challenges. Doing something seemingly easy but a bit dull, such as washing clothes, might be incredibly difficult for a person with ADHD to wrap their heads around.

→ **Disorganisation:** Forgetting appointments, dates and possessions, losing things, being fairly messy – these are all traits of a classic ADHD-er. Prioritising can be difficult, as our brains search for the most appealing thing to be doing at that point in time, so things like cleaning may simply not get done. ADHD-ers typically struggle with deadlines and simple organisation, because the small things can seem so overwhelming.

→ **Difficulty in completing projects:** In line with the above, it can be very difficult to complete a project when your attention won't play ball! We might also struggle with following instructions, as we might lose concentration halfway through and completely forget what they were, especially if they're not written down.

→ **Mental hyperactivity:** My brain feels like it is constantly racing with thoughts and simply will not be quiet. One way of describing it is as though you are a 'human doing' instead of a 'human being' – it feels impossible to not be always thinking about something. This can translate to anxiety and an overwhelming amount of thoughts and worries going on at any one time, which can also manifest as talking very quickly or excessively.

→ **Physical hyperactivity:** The mental aspects can translate to physical restlessness, where a person with ADHD may feel unable to sit still, as though they are being driven by a motor that makes them want to get up and walk around or fidget. This is where we often think of the screaming, hyper children most commonly associated with ADHD. In adults, it might be seen as insomnia.

→ **Impatience:** As our brains are moving so fast, ADHD-ers tend to be pretty impatient. This can result in interrupting others as they speak, having trouble waiting our turn or being impulsive, making decisions without fully thinking them out.

→ **Risky behaviour:** ADHD-ers may be prone to seeking out adrenaline in the form of risky decisions such as excessive spending, or self-medicating with alcohol or drugs. Our brains tend to be on the search for novel and exciting experiences, and we tend to get bored quickly.

→ **Mood swings and low self-esteem:** ADHD can be exhausting. Having the constant noise of thoughts in your head and seeming to upset people despite trying your absolute hardest often result in mood swings, from inspired highs to terrible lows. It can feel incredibly lonely having ADHD and as if nobody understands you. ADHD-ers often suffer from 'Rejection Sensitive Dysphoria'. We'll return to this topic later in the chapter 'R is for Rejection'.

As I'll show you in the chapter 'W is for Weaknesses', ADHD can also bring amazing benefits, such as:

→ **Creativity:** As we are literally cognitively diverse, ADHD-ers think outside of the box and tend to be extremely creative people, who excel at solving problems. Many of the world's leading creative thinkers have or may have had ADHD, such as Heston Blumenthal, Russell Brand, Olivia Attwood, Mel

B and will.i.am! People with ADHD are 300 per cent more likely to start their own business (LoPorto, 2005).

→ **Energy:** ADHD results in a lot of pent-up energy, which can lead to burnout, but can also be an amazing resource to draw upon, especially once we understand how to manage it.

→ **Bravery:** ADHD-ers tend to be fearless, in their decision-making, risk-taking and choices. As in 'E is for Executive Functioning', this can be due to the parts of our brains responsible for inhibition and fear being inhibited, which can lead us to just go for the things we want to do, like me writing this book!

→ **Authenticity:** When you have ADHD, you are motivated by passion and purpose, and whilst it can be very hard to find that purpose, it means that whatever you do, you will do it authentically, searching for true happiness.

→ **Kind-heartedness and compassion:** ADHD-ers generally care about others a great deal. In my experience, ADHD-ers have often faced difficulties which make us appreciate being sensitive and empathetic to others.

→ **Ability to multi-task:** Due to having several thoughts going on at the same time, people who have ADHD may be able to multi-task very well.

→ **Being calm in a crisis:** The adrenaline rush of a crisis can result in the ADHD brain being in a 'normal' mode, meaning we can be great in objectively stressful situations, such as emergencies. As in 'J is for Jobs', this can make us brilliantly suited to highly pressurised jobs, such as fire-fighting!

ADHD impacts the prefrontal cortex in our brains, which is responsible for thinking, thought analysis and regulating behaviour, essentially regulating our short- and long-term decision making. It helps us to focus our thoughts, pay attention and concentrate. It's the part that prevents us from eating chocolate ice-cream for breakfast, lunch and dinner every day, or ensures we do things that we might not particularly 'want' to do, like going to the gym on a cold morning before work. Essentially, it's the responsible, 'adult' part of our brain.

In ADHD-ers, the prefrontal cortex is unregulated, as I explain in 'E is for Executive Functioning'. There are no traffic lights slowing us down as we make decisions, no stabilisers on our imaginary bicycles preventing us from losing concentration and falling off as we become distracted by anything and everything. It can feel like having a Ferrari brain with bicycle brakes. The adult in the room preventing us from eating the ice cream for breakfast seems to have gone on holiday, which means we have to work much harder than other people at *not* doing the things we are inherently drawn towards, like scrolling through social media in the mornings or thinking about what to reply to a message from a friend. Things that aren't 'fun', like figuring out our bills, are much more difficult for us to do than for the average person.

Our judgement is also managed in the prefrontal cortex, including conceptualising how long it might take us to complete a task. Time management is typically affected by emotions here for ADHD-ers, who may feel more stressed at the thought of completing a task than they feel able to actually complete it. This is where procrastination, well known to ADHD-ers, enters the room. Whereas a person who doesn't have ADHD may be able to force themselves to 'get on with things', an ADHD-er may have to lock themselves in a room with no distractions in order to find the same level of motivation.

Emotions are regulated through this prefrontal cortex, which can explain the rapid mood changes that ADHD-ers are often accustomed to. We can often feel emotions very intensely, as though an emotion is the only thing we can focus on in any given moment, which can result in impulsivity. I think of this as being similar to how teenagers are written off as being 'hormonal' when they are emotional – ADHD-ers can find it much more difficult to control their emotions than others.

One of the reasons I didn't see ADHD as 'real' before being diagnosed was because I, like so many others, just thought I was being lazy and stupid. This is a big part of what prevents people from getting help with ADHD and at the same time makes it even worse to live with; we not only judge ADHD traits negatively, but we and others around us believe they are personal flaws. Being diagnosed is a huge act of compassion towards yourself, as you realise that the struggles you have encountered along the way are likely *because of your ADHD*. Not because you are stupid, lazy or weak – but because you are neurologically diverse.

Understanding your ADHD

When thinking about ADHD, a good starting point is to understand how it affects you overall and what your motivations are. ADHD-ers tend to struggle with things they inherently don't want to do and may devote too much attention to things they are interested in. By understanding what makes you 'tick', you can figure out how to hack your own brain to make those more tedious things a little bit easier!

1. Write down how ADHD has affected you so far in your life. Even if you haven't been diagnosed with it or aren't quite sure, try just writing down how you feel it could have possibly affected you. Try to approach this with a compassionate and kind mind towards yourself, accepting that this is a neurological condition that completely validates any difficulties you may have encountered as a result.

> For example, for me, my ADHD has impacted my ability to pay attention properly in lessons and has led to me making some very spontaneous decisions, such as deciding to move country! Now, I can accept this is part of my unique brain wiring, instead of beating myself up for it.

2. Make a list of five activities that you enjoy doing, and five things that you do not. Try to identify any similar themes between each category – for example, are the things you enjoy all exercise-based, or do they revolve around helping other people? Does the other list revolve around things that are repetitive or detail-orientated?

> I enjoy yoga, helping people, journaling, reading and dancing. Things I don't enjoy include managing my bills, taxes, maths, going to the post office and doing my clothes washing! The things I enjoy tend to be more based in emotions and connections, and the things I like less require me to be more detail-orientated and are less stimulating.

3. From this, assess your top three values – the things that motivate you in life. This could be love, validation, money, career achievements and so on.

> My top three values are helping others, being able to be myself (authenticity) and relationships with my friends and family.

4. Looking at these lists, try to identify three strengths – tools that you might typically use in the activities or values that are important to you. If you're not sure, ask some friends what they think your top three strengths are, or find an online personality test (e.g., VIA Character Strengths). These could include kindness, compassion, honesty, creativity and so on.

> My top three strengths are creativity, kindness and curiosity.

5. Assess how much of your life you are currently living in line with your strengths, values and activities you enjoy. Are there ways that you can increase the time spent on doing the things you enjoy?

> I probably spend a bit too much time working, and not enough time seeing people I care about, so I'll put in boundaries, such as having a maximum number of coaching clients at one time.

6. Now look at the list of activities that you do not enjoy doing and try to figure out a way to make them align with your values. For example, if you're motivated by friendship, could you set up an 'accountability buddy' to check in on how many administrative tasks you've completed each week?

> I'm motivated by friends and family, so I'll try to take a walk
> with them so I get outside during winter!

7. Make a plan of three specific goals you might have that
   are related to your ADHD, and how you can achieve these.
   For example, you might want to stop making impulsive
   decisions, so a corresponding action could be to seek out
   a therapist or write down your decisions at the end of each
   day. Give yourself a generous timeline!

   > I want to make sure I take the time to cook food each week so
   > I don't skip meals, so I'll plan meals, organise a regular food
   > shop delivery, and schedule time in my diary to cook each
   > weekend.

is for Burnout

Did you know?

- Adults are usually diagnosed with ADHD after a burnout. It has been suggested that people with ADHD have had to put in 500 per cent more effort than average throughout childhood and exams, and just assumed everyone had to work as hard as they did (Ross, 2016).

- There is research to suggest that career success could be compromised by having ADHD, and that there are clear weaknesses in the UK and internationally at addressing occupational difficulties (Adamou et al., 2013).

- Adolescent girls with ADHD were found to be significantly more likely to attempt suicide or injure themselves than those who do not have ADHD (American Psychological Association (APA), 2012).

Burnout is commonly seen in ADHD-ers. It is the result of exhaustion and trying to meet unrealistic expectations, often self-imposed! ADHD-ers tend to have a lot of excess energy, especially when starting something new or when they are inspired, which can see them working at incredible rates – a consequence of our ability to hyper-focus!

This effort level is generally unsustainable in the long run. This can be frustrating and de-motivating for the ADHD-er in question, who can beat themselves up for not being able to maintain this unrealistic energy. Our brains are simply not designed to run at this level of concentration for very long, but it can feel like we should be able to, simply because we sometimes can. It can contribute to feeling as though ADHD isn't a 'real' neurodevelopmental condition, because we wrongly assume we can concentrate if we 'put our minds to it'; unfortunately, it's often the other way round – our ADHD minds choose what we are able to concentrate on.

Burnout can come in many different forms. Physically, it can leave a person utterly exhausted to the point of illness, as their bodies simply shut down in an effort to make them stop. It might manifest as panic attacks or migraines. Mentally, this could mean getting caught in a spiral of guilt and self-hatred, resulting in cancelling plans or quitting commitments, and being mentally depleted to the point of total exhaustion.

The core concept for ADHD-ers to bear in mind is that **YOU CANNOT DO IT ALL.** Despite feeling that you can achieve anything that you put your mind to at the outset, it is so important to remind yourself that you are a human being like everybody else.

Counteracting burnout requires us to slow down and consider the reasons behind these feelings. The following factors can often contribute to the temptation to over-exert yourself:

Insecurity

It is quite ironic that ADHD-ers may often place themselves under serious pressure to perform because of insecurities which stem from being unable to perform fully in the past. Placing unrealistic expectations on ourselves will usually mean that we are unable to meet them, which can lead to a lack of trust and low self-esteem. We also tend to be more sensitive to rejection, often suffering from 'Rejection Sensitive Dysphoria' (see 'R is for Rejection' for more on this), having likely been told off as a child for being neurologically diverse. Finally, our tendency to make impulsive decisions can often result in negative experiences or being unable to commit, which all leads to more pressure when we try the next time.

Whenever I feel insecure, my coping mechanism tends to be forging ahead with new ideas and pushing myself to work harder than usual. Ironically, despite working harder than usual to prove myself, other people may not respond to the extra level of effort being put in as expected, which in turn can lead to further insecurity and a further determination to work harder – until I hit burnout! Just because we can push ourselves to work 24 hours a day doesn't mean everybody else will be able to keep up with us.

To tackle insecurities, it is good to make a list of any potential triggers and identify areas of your life where this could be an issue and how you react. This will help ensure that you are acting from a confident, assured place, instead of out of fear.

Personal boundaries

ADHD doesn't go particularly well with boundaries, which can be thought of as traffic lights – we may tend to zoom past them without stopping. Boundaries are guidelines, rules or limits that may be set by society, other people or ourselves, identifying how to behave in different situations.

Setting, upholding and respecting boundaries require us to stop and think before acting, self-regulating our behaviour.

As in 'E is for Executive Functioning', ADHD-ers may struggle with things such as self-awareness, inhibition, time management and emotional regulation, which can mean we sometimes simply don't even recognise or process boundaries.

For example, I really struggle to follow rules if I don't believe in them or see the purpose behind them, especially arbitrary ones, such as having to check work with lots of specific people before handing it in as finished.

This can result in us burning ourselves out, as these seemingly bureaucratic processes are often in place for a reason. For example, crossing roads at pedestrian crossings might seem frustrating when there are no cars to be seen, but cars can suddenly appear out of nowhere. If we all ignored the road crossings, there'd be endless accidents!

This can also apply in situations involving the boundaries we set (or don't!) for ourselves. For example, if I wake up in the night, I might simply get up and start working instead of going back to sleep, despite this meaning I'll feel very unwell in the daytime.

As we can struggle with self-awareness, we might find ourselves being unaware of how much we're already taking on in terms of work and how much energy we have to do other things. This can result in us automatically saying yes to things, as in chapter 'N is for No', which leads to us trying to uphold too many commitments to different people and burning out!

Hyper-focus, impatience and unrealistic expectations

People who have ADHD may need to do everything *right*

now whilst they can, because they want to do everything this minute. In my experience, we tend to have two categories for assessing time: 'now' and 'not now'. The concept of waiting, of things taking place over a few months as opposed to a few weeks, is difficult to imagine. This can cause feelings of insecurity – that maybe you won't be there in a few months to be able to do it, so it needs to be done right now.

If we are on the high of an exciting new project, we might also be overly optimistic about how much energy we think we want to commit to this project at the start. It can be difficult to slow down the excited adrenaline and think about things in a long-term way, and to accurately assess our own capabilities. ADHD-ers may find themselves setting unrealistically short deadlines for work projects, for example, despite issues with time management being one of the main symptoms of ADHD!

Ultimately, burnout comes from over-committing yourself to too many things. It stems from problems with pausing, thinking and assessing before acting, as in 'E is for Executive Functioning'.

Self-fulfilling prophecy

Many people live by 'stories', which are beliefs such as 'I am not good enough to do X, Y or Z'. It can sometimes be easier to fulfil this prophecy than to take a risk by actually applying ourselves and seeing what happens. It may feel easier to steamroll ahead in a flurry of ideas and feel like you have some control over your situation, even if it involves sabotaging it, than to be vulnerable enough to admit you don't know everything, to ask for help and learn from others.

Lack of trust in both others and ourselves can cause us to make decisions which lead to burnout, such as pushing ourselves to extremes.

Adrenaline

As our brains are seeking dopamine and excitement, we can often overwork ourselves due to the way our brains feel when we're 'doing' things. This can lead to us becoming 'human doings' instead of human beings, where we simply work non-stop. Our society is unfortunately highly geared to what we 'do', rather than who we are, which can drive us to become addicted to feeling as though we're doing something 'useful'.

This can feel counterintuitive to having ADHD, especially because of the stigma related to ADHD-ers struggling with completing tasks. However, on the opposite end of the spectrum, we can push ourselves to extremes in completing certain tasks and completely ignoring others, such as resting!

I can often find myself automatically prioritising working above self-care activities such as showering, cooking, exercising or eating meals, especially if I'm hyper-focusing. Though I might feel 'productive' if I spend an entire day glued to my laptop, the work I'm doing is unlikely to be very good quality, as breaks are vitally important for our brains to work properly.

For me, doing 'nothing' and relaxing can feel extremely uncomfortable, as my brain is constantly whirring away with new ideas and pushing me to try to do them all at once. I once went to a Workaholics Anonymous meeting and found it ironic that over half of the other attendees had ADHD!

Seeking out adrenaline and dopamine highs to an unhealthy degree like this can lead to us becoming very unwell. It's important to get professional help if you're experiencing serious issues with this and it is something I often work on with clients.

Ways to deal with burnout

The best way to deal with the cycle of burnout is to plan ahead.

1. First, notice when the cycle starts. Think about times in the past when you may have over-committed yourself and burned out, then try to spot the thing that links them together, such as stress.

    > For example, I burned out whilst writing books or trying to cram an entire law degree in my head in one month! The thing that links these things together is setting myself impossible deadlines, creating a very stressful environment.

2. Once you have your triggers, try to see how your burnout cycle plays out. Do you say yes to too many invitations, or make sure you are the last one in the office each night? Do you start new hobbies? Try to find the warning signs. Write down the things you do when you find yourself on the burnout rollercoaster.

    > I over-commit to doing too many things at the same time and stop doing basic self-care like cooking or exercise.

3. Now, identify the negative things that have happened when you have burned yourself out before. Do you feel that you have let people down, or have you become physically

unwell? Have you quit projects or plans, or simply cut people off?

> My relationships with others have really suffered, and I become physically exhausted.

4. Think about the things you have done in the past and try to feel the emotions connected with those actions. Accept however you feel – whether that is guilt, shame, embarrassment or anything else – and try to give yourself some love. Write down a little note of encouragement to yourself to find the positives, even if it is just being able to reach this point. Maybe you want to say an apology to your body or gently acknowledge that situations may have been objectively different to how you perceived them emotionally at the time. Remember that you have only ever done the best with the resources you had available to you at the time.

> I apologise to myself for the many gruelling workdays I've put myself through, unrealistic standards I've held myself to, and the impact this has had on my health.

5. Identify how you have burned out before and how you have felt better afterwards. Write down the things that make you happy and feel relaxed, such as exercise or journaling – these are your coping strategies.

> I've burned out previously by losing a lot of weight, having panic attacks and having fights with my friends and family. I've felt better by having a holiday, taking breaks, journaling, going to therapy and doing yoga.

6. Write down the ways you can stop yourself becoming burned out in the future, such as:

- Setting yourself limits and deciding how many hours per week you want to work, socialise, do hobbies and relax.

- Giving yourself 'time cushions' between appointments and meetings.

- Creating a schedule for yourself, with a set time for breaks and to stop working each day – with reminders!

- Scheduling time for yourself each week, such as having one evening free at a minimum.

- Setting yourself rules such as not meeting up with more than one person per day – and sticking to them!

- Get help with administrative tasks, for example, from a virtual assistant (Access to Work can fund these!). They can be particularly helpful at saying 'no' on your behalf if this is something you struggle with.

- Attending Workaholic Anonymous meetings if you find a persistent issue with working too much. There's a strong correlation between workaholism and ADHD (Robinson, 2014).

- Having a 'burnout buddy' to share this plan with, so they can intervene if they spot some of the signs of you potentially burning yourself out – you can offer to do the same for them!

Your plan is there to help you spot the triggers of potential burnout and to act before it happens. Every person with ADHD is different and will have different ways of coping best with stress.

Ultimately, the main thing to work on is self-compassion and self-worth, and confidence in yourself, which we will see in the next chapter. It is only when you are kind to yourself that you can turn up *as you are* with a simple confidence in that whatever you produce at a healthy level will be great. It is the confidence in knowing that you have time and that you will make the right decisions for yourself in the future, that you do not have to do everything, and other people's happiness is their responsibility. You can say no, put yourself first and still be accepted.

is for Confidence

Did you know?

- There is evidence to suggest that ADHD is associated with lower self-esteem in adulthood (Cook *et al.*, 2014).

- It has been suggested that for every 15 negative comments a child with ADHD receives, there is only one positive comment (Saline, 2019).

- It's estimated about 18.6 per cent of adults are affected by both ADHD and depression (CHADD, 2019).

Confidence is an elusive concept for ADHD-ers. For me it comes in waves. One moment I'll have total confidence in my own ideas, thinking creatively and fearlessly taking risks, the next I'll come crashing down with perceived rejection, failures and insecurities. It can be quite complicated for people to understand how one moment you can be so overly confident, and the next so crippled with insecurity that you cancel all of your plans.

Overall, I believe that most people who have ADHD suffer from low self-esteem on some level, no matter how confident or successful they seem on the outside.

This can come from our childhood experiences. ADHD is developmental, so our early years are considered as part of the diagnostic process, to assess how we may have been impacted throughout our lives. Thinking differently makes you different, which is no fun as a child just wanting to fit in. It might mean that you are bullied for your enthusiasm, told off for interrupting, chastised for not being able to pay attention in class, or find it hard to make friends. It might mean that the things you really love as a child, you are made to feel bad at, and take this to mean that *you* are bad. These childhood experiences form our fundamental beliefs about ourselves and how we interact with others in the world.

As the parts of our brains responsible for inhibition, emotion and self-awareness are impacted by ADHD (see 'E is for Executive Functioning'), this can result in us fearlessly and impulsively taking huge risks. It's only later, when our emotions kick in, that we might feel completely overwhelmed with these decisions and beat ourselves up for them!

In this way, we can suffer from imposter syndrome, especially because we think so differently to neurotypical people.

For example, I never felt intelligent growing up, because I learned differently to everybody else – and yet I never felt like I could admit I had a problem because I was objectively 'successful' in the eyes of others. I didn't feel that I deserved my good exam marks, because I was unable to concentrate throughout the year during classes, instead teaching myself the entire subject the week before an exam. I felt like I had cheated somehow, by learning differently – my teachers even asked my classmates if I had cheated when I got straight As, which didn't help!

ADHD does not fit neatly inside the lines of the society that we have prescribed ourselves, which we are first introduced to as children. Having a neurodivergent brain means you think differently to others, but schools dictate certain ways of behaving, measurements of success and boxes to fit into. Our society prizes exam results and having a good 'status' job over whether we enjoy it, meaning that many people may be living a life that is not authentic to them. Having ADHD can make it impossible to fit into the box, but it doesn't mean that you are the problem.

Building confidence and self-esteem is critical to thriving with ADHD. Having ADHD can feel at odds with being confident, but once you learn how to manage this and grow confident in yourself, it can become your superpower. Energy, inspiration and creativity are all common traits of people who have ADHD. This means that you have powers that other people do not. Being different is your superpower – this is what should give you confidence, knowing that you see the world in a unique way and that you have a way of thinking that other people do not have.

Self-acceptance is the first step to confidence

Having ADHD in a neurotypical world can lead us to beat ourselves up for not being 'normal'. In a world where humans are now supposed to be able to sit still for hours on end in front of screens, it's hardly surprising that our brains are still seeking out stimulation beyond what we're told 'should' be enough.

If you compare your ability to do things such as manage time or regulate your attention to neurotypical people, you will always find yourself coming up short. This isn't because you're 'bad' at certain things; it's just the way your brain is wired. In the right situation, you can harness your ADHD to do exceptional things – but only after letting go of trying to be 'normal'. Instead of focusing on what's wrong, focus on what's right – your unique strengths, abilities and passions. It might sound cheesy, but if you feel like you don't fit in this world, it's because you're here to help create a new one. Accepting that you have ADHD is the first step to increasing your confidence. When we own who we are, we understand what we're working with. My life changed when I was diagnosed with ADHD because I finally allowed myself to feel self-compassion and acknowledge the pain that I had felt throughout my life at being different, lazy and stupid – for something that was always out of my control. It helped me see that there was a reason for being the way I was; accepting that I have ADHD gave me the keys to unlock myself. I stopped trying to fit myself into a neurotypical box and beating myself up for not being able to think how I was 'supposed' to, instead freeing myself to think in my own way.

Low self-esteem can affect us in many ways – whether that is how productive we are, how we look, how popular we are or anything else we may feel insecure about. The irony is that insecure people often react to this by overcompensating (see 'B is for Burnout'!), but you might recognise patterns of acting out against your insecurities in yourself.

True confidence comes from knowing that you are enough, exactly as you are. You do not need to change yourself to fit in. You do not need to apologise for being who you are, for how productive you are, or for taking up space in the world. Having ADHD is not a burden to the people around you. It is just part of who you are, and that is simply a human being.

One thing that taught me to be a little kinder to myself is to picture a baby. The baby is loved simply for existing – it does not have to do anything, or be anyone in particular, to be deemed worthy of love. It actually can cry all day and be a fairly big nuisance, yet it is still loved all the same. You just love them regardless of anything else. That is the love that people feel towards you – whether you want to acknowledge it or not.

The secret to feeling confident is to be compassionate to yourself. Don't set yourself up for failure. If you feel confident, you are guaranteed to do a better job.

Having ADHD can feel like a hindrance to being confident, because there is a lot to be aware of in terms of how it can impact you. However, if you refuse to apologise for who you are, you are already winning. Accepting yourself and all of the quirks that you come with is half the battle. Acknowledging these quirks allows you to truly accept them as a positive part of who you are.

Dealing with insecurity

Overcoming insecurity comes with noticing how we talk about ourselves and the inner voice that is narrating our life. I didn't realise this until a friend pointed out how horrible I was being to myself on a daily basis, always putting myself down and calling myself ugly. I would never dream of speaking like that to anybody else.

Nowadays I try to be very mindful of what I say about myself around anyone, but an excellent way to think of your own insecurity is to imagine that it is flowing out to the people around you. Imagine a mother calling herself fat in front of her daughter – who only sees a strong, beautiful woman in front of her but inherits the fear of being 'fat'. When you call yourself stupid around your friends – all of whom think you are an intelligent, brilliant person – this will trigger their own insecurities. We all have them! It's brilliantly captured in the scene in the movie *Mean Girls*, where the young women berate themselves in the mirror as a form of toxic bonding, the insecurity flowing from one character to the next.

Capitalism feeds off us feeling bad about ourselves, thriving on insecurities. If everyone in the world woke up tomorrow and was happy with how they looked, billion-pound industries would come crashing down overnight.

Choose to beat the system and to be confident in yourself. I can say with total 'confidence' that literally nobody cares about what you are doing – they are all far too busy worrying about themselves. Notice how you feel about other people and remember that is probably how they feel about you. If you try something and fail, nobody will think worse of you for it – they will most likely just forget within a few days.

You are the only person who cares about what you do, at the end of the day. Your confidence ultimately only matters to you. You aren't going to reach your deathbed and care about the things that your acquaintances got up to in their twenties, or all of the times you held yourself back. Perfection is impossible – our mistakes and 'failures' are what make up our successes, teaching us new things every time. By embracing yourself and being your own biggest supporter, regardless of how many times you fall down, you can live your life with confidence and happiness.

How to beat insecurity

1. Identify what negative opinions you might have about yourself and why you think they are a problem. If none

spring mind, think about what makes you feel really angry, then look behind that – why do you feel angry? Have a think about why you feel these insecurities and where they come from. For example, feeling 'bad' at managing bills, and linking this back to struggling in maths classes at school. Note what impact this insecurity has on your life – for example, does it prevent you from taking up certain opportunities?

> For example, I feel insecure about public speaking, having burst into tears in front of the class whilst doing it at school! As a result, I don't put myself forward to speak to large audiences as much as I could, because I feel scared of doing it in 'real life'. If I have to do it, I get extremely stressed the night before.

2. (Don't do this exercise straightaway for everything on your list. Tackle them one at a time, and only move on to the next one when you feel ready.) First, write the opposite statement down and all of the proof to back it up, such as 'I am good at managing bills. Proof of this includes having certain bills in my name, the supply of which has never been cut off!'

> I am good at public speaking. Proof of this includes speaking in front of people every day, having spoken in panel events, and having given presentations to companies like Microsoft!

3. Identify ways that you can target this insecurity in a practical way. This might involve looking at the problem itself and acknowledging areas where you could use some help. For example, asking a friend how they set up standing orders for bills to be paid automatically each month.

> I know speaking in front of a physical audience by myself feels scary, so I can go to Toast Masters events and practise or try a stand-up comedy course.

4. Dedicate some time to putting your method into action – for example, scheduling an hour at the end of a month to go through your bills and ensure they are all in order.

> I can find a course to go to that will help me with speaking in front of people and dedicate one evening per week to it.

5. Write yourself a positive statement about the insecurity, such as 'I am in full control of my finances', and stick this on your bathroom mirror for a week.

> 'I am a great public speaker.'

6. Return to this exercise regularly, especially whenever you notice that you are feeling particularly insecure about something. Remember that everybody has insecurities and the trick to beating them is acknowledging that they are simply stories we are telling ourselves!

> I do public speaking all the time, so having this insecurity feels very irrational!

How to grow your confidence

1. Write down a list of 30 of your achievements so far in life, no matter how small – these can definitely include 'getting out of bed on cold days' and 'finishing school'!

> For example, publishing this book, learning how to do a headstand in a yoga class, becoming an ADHD coach.

2. Identify your top five strengths – you could do this by

assessing yourself, asking other people or doing an online personality quiz. Once you have your top five, look at how much you are using your strengths on a daily basis. Try to think of ways you could increase this.

> Mine are curiosity, creativity, kindness, authenticity and compassion.

3. Think about how someone who loves you would describe you. What impact have you had in their life?

> Someone said I have been their 'biggest inspiration and completely transformed how I see my ADHD!'

4. Appoint a 'confidence friend'. Ask them to call you out every time you speak badly of yourself and note it down. Write the opposite proof down for every negative statement you say.

5. Spot what makes you feel insecure – is it talking to a certain person or scrolling on social media? Decide to limit this in your life and notice the difference, for example, by staying off social media for a day. Make a conscious effort to stop comparing yourself to other people.

> Social media makes me feel insecure, so I turn off all my notifications and have deleted the apps from my phone home screen.

is for Diagnosis

Did you know?

- There is no biological test for ADHD, so the diagnosis is made on the basis of a full developmental and psychiatric history, observer reports and examination of the mental state by a qualified specialist. (National Collaborating Centre for Mental Health, 2009).

- The waiting list for an ADHD assessment in the UK can be up to seven years in some areas (BBC News, 2018). Around a third of people are thought to have waited over two years before being formally diagnosed (Born to Be ADHD, 2017).

- In July 2020, Freedom of Information requests to NHS trusts found at least 21,000 adults on waiting lists for ADHD services (Lindsay, 2020).

Being diagnosed with ADHD can be a very overwhelming and complicated process. There are very long waiting lists in the UK for assessments under the NHS, and private psychiatrists can be extremely expensive. However, it is important to know that you have a legal right to choose the specialist to whom your GP refers you.

If your doctor agrees that you might have ADHD and wishes to refer you to a specialist for assessment, you can ask to be referred to Psychiatry-UK[1] (or any other qualified provider). As they are based online, assessments can happen much more quickly than having to wait for an in-person appointment.

1   https://psychiatry-uk.com/right-to-choose

For more information about this, I strongly recommend looking at the resources of a charity called ADHD UK, who provide sample letters that you can send to your doctor.[2]

For me, being diagnosed was not only helpful for treatment purposes, such as medication, but also because of how liberating it was to accept that I had a neurodevelopmental condition, instead of beating myself up for things that were not within my control. It felt enormously validating to have a 'reason' for feeling so different throughout my life.

However, being diagnosed can also be an emotional rollercoaster and it is important to remember that, ultimately, it is one person's assessment: you are still the same person either way.

It's important to remember that ADHD symptoms can commonly overlap or coexist with other conditions and be misdiagnosed. For example, ADHD has been strongly linked to Autism, dyslexia, dyscalculia, anxiety, depression, eating disorders and sleep disorders. Most of my coaching clients have experienced at least one of these conditions accompanying their ADHD. Many of them, particularly the women, have experienced a string of medical misdiagnoses, as in 'X is for X-treme Differences in Women'.

There is a general lack of awareness about ADHD and the stigma attached to it, even amongst professionals. Because it manifests differently in everybody, it can be extremely hard to diagnose and even specialists might have different opinions. Existing systemic racial inequities and biases in

---

2   https://adhduk.co.uk/wp-content/uploads/sites/6/2o21/o4/ADHD-UK-Letter-to-GP-s-on-Right-to-Choose.pdf

our society also apply – Asian, Black and Hispanic children are significantly less likely to be diagnosed with ADHD or receive treatment for it, compared with White children (Shi *et al.*, 2021).

This is in contrast to the overload of information about ADHD online. As an ADHD coach, I've lost count of how many people told me they self-diagnosed from seeing social media posts. Content on social media can be over-simplified to become as relatable as possible and can be distorted by algorithms and targeted advertising. For example, adverts by a medical company linking ADHD with obesity were removed from Instagram and TikTok in 2022 for promoting a negative body image (Urian, 2022). I speak about this more in my book on social media, *The Reality Manifesto* (Maskell, 2022).

I strongly recommend seeking out a diagnosis from a reputable, licensed psychiatrist. Remember that if you don't agree with the assessment of one specialist, you have options, and I would advise seeking other opinions until you find one you feel accurately reflects your situation.

If you disagree with the assessment, you could explain why to the specialist, and ask for a referral to somebody else for a second opinion. Alternatively, you could reach out to another specialist yourself.

As there can be so much money involved in paying for private assessments for ADHD, you could ask how many people *aren't* diagnosed after an assessment. You're also entitled to ask how the psychiatrist has reached their opinion and can look at the process for complaints if you believe there's a serious issue.

Ultimately, what you choose to believe is down to you, and nobody knows your brain better than you do.

My experience of diagnosis

After graduating from university, I was very overwhelmed trying to figure out 'what to do with my life', repeatedly making erratic, impulsive and self-sabotaging decisions. I just thought that this was me being unable to cope with the 'real world', but I became extremely depressed and anxious as a result.

A year later, my life was an utter mess. I had very toxic relationships, kept arguing with people, was dependent on alcohol and kept spontaneously booking flights to move country as a way of dealing with my problems. I felt like I didn't fit into society, couldn't keep a job or make any basic decisions, even on where to live, and would wake up afraid of what I might do by the end of the day.

Finally, I googled how I was feeling and self-diagnosed myself with *everything* I found (except ADHD!). I was terrified and convinced that I'd be sectioned if I told anybody what I was experiencing.

Eventually, I hit what I thought was 'rock bottom' and went to see a counsellor, feeling the most intense amount of shame and fear. Then I was angry to be told that I was paying £70 for somebody just to listen to me, and she couldn't diagnose me with anything or even tell me what she thought!

I visited many different doctors with my symptoms over the course of the next year when things became unbearable.

The doctors refused to acknowledge that I had any problems other than possible 'emotional issues', because I appeared extremely 'self-aware, intelligent and was not about to rob a bank'. Which was a relief to hear in the moment, but very worrying as I walked out knowing that something had been missed. It felt like I was making a fuss out of nothing, just going to the doctor for being lazy and stupid.

Part of why being diagnosed is so hard is because it takes so much bravery to even acknowledge that you need help and then to go to a doctor in the first place to ask for this. It can be even harder if the doctor is saying what you ultimately want to hear – that you're fine – and you need to prove to them that they are wrong.

I became obsessed with researching different mental health conditions to try to fill in the doctor's mistakes, which later developed into suicidal ideation. This was really scary to experience, and eventually I visited a private psychiatrist to try to get help.

The session cost approximately £400 for one hour. I listed all my problems and he stopped me to ask, 'Do you have problems concentrating? Do you find that you interrupt people often, and cannot stick at anything for very long?'

The questions he asked were all very relevant to my problems and described my life, but I had never thought about things in that way before. Eventually, he said, 'You have ADHD. Nothing else.' I burst out laughing and said, 'ADHD is fine! That's not a real problem!', asking for what I saw as 'socially acceptable' medication.

The psychiatrist said that ADHD could not be diagnosed

in one session, though I clearly had it, and very badly so. I was told to return for another £400 session, where he would assess the impacts on my life up to that point. However, I didn't return for an entire year because I spontaneously moved abroad whilst on holiday the next week! This is another hurdle for people with ADHD in being diagnosed – we might not have stable enough lives to even have GPs, let alone live in the same place whilst waiting months or years for an assessment.

Fortunately, I later returned to the UK and to the psychiatrist, knowing that I ultimately needed professional help. Although I felt embarrassed for not being able to deal with it by myself, I finally believed that ADHD was most definitely real.

On this second session, I was asked another long list of questions, and was given two forms to have filled out by family members or friends who had known me since childhood. This part of the process can be upsetting but is ultimately really important, especially because we struggle with self-awareness and memory, as in 'E is for Executive Functioning'. However, this means that other people may remember things differently to us, and it might feel distressing to revisit our previous experiences with this new perspective.

After I provided the forms, the psychiatrist prescribed me with medication, which was life-changing in helping me to manage my symptoms, as discussed further in 'M is for Medication'. I was shocked to learn, however, that I would have to pay £300 per month to have this prescription *for the rest of my life.*

This was because the prescription had been provided by a private psychiatrist. For this to be provided by the NHS, I was told that I'd need to have my diagnosis confirmed again and could face potential gaps in treatment. I was extremely overwhelmed at the thought of going through this process again, and the money I'd already spent being wasted, but I simply couldn't afford it.

It felt like a tax on being neurodiverse and a ridiculous sum of money to pay just for the privilege of being able to function like other people were able to. It also made me question my entire diagnosis and whether I was being exploited financially, as I was already very scared of becoming 'addicted' to the medication.

I asked the psychiatrist to write a letter to my GP, as it seemed better in the long run to wait for another assessment on the NHS than to be locked into paying so much money forever. However, I was shocked to learn from my GP that they could continue prescribing me medication from this diagnosis whilst waiting for the confirmation through their own routes, which took a few months, and was very similar in terms of the substantive process.

Since then, I've had a collaborative and transparent approach to treatment with my GP, which has worked much better. Nevertheless, if I want to change my medication to be higher than what I've been prescribed privately, I'd need to be assessed by a specialist again. My current surgery told me their NHS waiting list was seven years – I definitely don't think I'd be here today if I'd had to wait that long.

I recognise how privileged I am to have been able to access

treatment, which is why I wrote this book, to share my experiences with others in the hope that it can help them and raise awareness of the terrible situations so many of us face in accessing support. No one should have to go through this process to receive the help they're entitled to, which can often be confusing, upsetting, demoralising, expensive and exploitative, even if it's worth it in the end.

What you might experience

Even just thinking about whether you may have ADHD, let alone being assessed and diagnosed with it, can be extremely overwhelming. I'd strongly recommend seeking the support of a therapist throughout this process who can help you process some of the feelings that might arise, which are discussed below.

Excitement

Learning about ADHD is exciting, as you can finally piece together your experiences in life. No, you're not weird, stupid or lazy! You are just neurodiverse! You might become hyper-focused on ADHD and talk to others a lot about it, expecting them to share your elation and relief.

As people with ADHD often attract others with similar personalities (we don't mind each other interrupting!), you might also be tempted to 'diagnose' others. Remember that you cannot diagnose anyone and are (probably!) not a medical professional qualified in making such assessments, so try to resist telling someone that they might have ADHD! If someone asks you whether you think they have it, advise them to speak to their doctor.

Though it is exciting, try not to attach too much of your identity to ADHD: you're still the same person, you can just have a bit more compassion for yourself now! It's also good to be careful about being selective in who you speak to about it, such as only those who know you well and whom you trust.

Loneliness/sadness

This process can bring a lot of memories up from throughout your life when you felt misunderstood or struggled because of your ADHD. You may also be able to understand the impact it has had on your relationships and feel isolated, overwhelmed and scared.

Input from your family and friends during the assessment process can be distressing, especially if you don't have strong lifelong relationships with others, possibly due to having ADHD! Your loved ones may also be anxious about the assessment, as they can remember your experiences differently, especially if you were able to hide your struggles.

ADHD also comes with a lot of stigma and it can feel very lonely if the people around you do not 'believe' in it. If this is the case, I advise reaching out to support groups, as in 'U is for Unite', to connect with others having similar experiences. It helps to have at least one person in your life to support you throughout this process, so please do try to find someone to talk to about what you are experiencing.

Being diagnosed with a neurodevelopmental condition does force you to realise that you are different from others, but you are not alone in this.

Fear

Thinking about ADHD can be scary, especially if you're not used to thinking about your 'mental health' and life experiences. Trying to figure out medical services and talking about your feelings to medical professionals can be very scary, but I promise it is worth it!

It might also feel scary to talk to other people about this, especially if you've been diagnosed later in life. For example, it can be confusing to think about whether to disclose this at work, as in 'J is for Jobs', or who 'needs' to know. You might find yourself questioning how this diagnosis might change your life, but remember that there's no rush to decide anything. This also applies to things such as medication – I felt very scared to start taking it at first and asked lots of people for their advice instead of thinking about what was best for me. You are not alone in what you are experiencing and being diagnosed with ADHD[3] (or anything else!) does not change who you are. All it does is allow you to understand yourself better and receive treatment for any difficulties you are experiencing. That treatment won't change who you are either: it will just make your life easier.

Anger

Anger is normal to experience, especially when you realise that you may have been struggling for a long time with something that was never within your control. The diagnosis process can also be so complicated, expensive and generally un-ADHD-friendly that it can also be very anger-inducing.

---

3   https://members.adhdunlocked.co.uk/~access/a1c91f

It might feel frustrating to try to talk to other people about this, or as though they don't understand, but it's very important to remember that everybody is doing the best they can with what they have available to them.

Professionals' understanding of ADHD and the diagnostic criteria is very different now to 20 years ago. With this in mind, I can understand why my ADHD wasn't picked up on earlier. For example, my parents took me to the doctor because I seemed unable to listen and concentrate as a child, and the doctor said this was due to a build-up of earwax. Although it can feel confronting to imagine your life if you'd been diagnosed earlier, it's advisable to focus your energy as much as possible on your future with this newfound knowledge. The dots often only make sense when we look backwards!

Happiness

Overall, you will hopefully reach a point where you feel happy and peaceful, and experience self-acceptance and empowerment. Ultimately, ADHD comes with many brilliant aspects, such as compassion, creativity and fun. Being diagnosed simply gives us additional knowledge about who we are and empowers us to live in the ways we want to, rather than trying to squish ourselves into neurotypical ways of living.

If you are diagnosed, your doctor should have a 'structured discussion' with you about how ADHD can affect your life (National Institute for Health and Care Excellence, 2019). Treatment is generally holistic, so may include talking therapy, medication and/or lifestyle changes, such as exercise. The overall point is for you to be happy and healthy.

Being diagnosed with ADHD was by far the best thing to ever happen to me, as I was able to finally take control of my life and live it how I wanted to, instead of trying to survive in a maelstrom of daily chaos.

How to get an ADHD assessment in the UK as an adult

→   If you think that you may have ADHD and would like an assessment, fill in an accredited online symptom checklist,[4] and take this to your GP. Be prepared to explain your symptoms and why you think you have ADHD honestly.

→   If your GP agrees that you may have ADHD, they can refer you to a specialist for assessment. Ask your GP about typical waiting times, and if you'd like to, ask to be referred to Psychiatry-UK,[5] exercising your 'right to choose' under the NHS Constitution[6] (if based in England).

→   Depending on your specific situation, you might wish to visit a private psychiatrist for an appointment. If you can, tell your GP about your plans and ask them whether they will be able to accept the referral from a private psychiatrist. They may be able to recommend one to you and write a letter of support. Look at different options and price ranges!

→   Ask a couple of people that you trust to support you in this

4   https://add.org/wp-content/uploads/2015/03/adhd-questionnaire-ASRS111.pdf

5   Follow the instructions here if relevant: https://psychiatry-uk.com/right-to-choose

6   NHS Gateway Publication number 07661, 'Choice in Mental Health Care', updated in February 2018.

process, including accompanying you to any appointments or providing background information if required.

→ When you visit the psychiatrist for an assessment, make sure that you are well prepared. Try to find any school reports you may still have that present a full picture of how ADHD may have impacted you throughout your life.

→ If you are diagnosed privately, ask to be referred back to the NHS once you have been diagnosed, and for a copy of your diagnosis and any prescriptions that you may be given. If your assessment is on the NHS, your GP might be provided with the results directly, and should update you accordingly.

→ Ask your GP to refer you to a therapist for support throughout this process or consider finding your own if this is not possible, preferably one with experience in ADHD.

It may be that you are unable to be diagnosed with ADHD for one reason or another, and it might not be necessary if you have lived your life until now with relatively few problems. ADHD-ers tend to be very resourceful and develop amazing coping mechanisms throughout their life. Although it can be helpful to have the confirmation from a medical professional, it's not always necessary unless you are looking to gain something specific from the diagnosis. If this is the case, I would recommend just remaining open to the possibility that you may have some aspects of ADHD and taking what you need from this book. It is difficult, but try not to overthink it!

There are several lifestyle changes as set out in this book that you can make to treat symptoms that do not require you to be diagnosed. See those listed in 'M is for Medication'.

Above all, remember that having ADHD, or any other neurodivergent condition, does *not* mean that there is 'something wrong with you'. It is simply just part of who you are, just like your height or eye colour.

These conditions are ultimately thought up by humans and given to us as labels. We are all human beings with a huge range of emotions and brain activity. There is so much we have yet to learn about ADHD, and being diagnosed with it simply allows you to know yourself better and *receive the help that you deserve*. It does not make you weak – it makes you strong.

If this chapter has made you feel emotional at the difficulties in receiving help that someone in this position may experience, please talk about it as much as you can. Raise awareness, write to your local MP, speak to your GP or people that you know.

If you have someone with ADHD in your life and are looking for information on how to support them throughout this process, please try to remember to just accept them as they are and be there for them unconditionally. It's helpful if you can give your advice when asked for it, but remember that the person might be feeling very overwhelmed, and extra-sensitive to your opinions about their experiences. Being reminded that we are loved, regardless of having ADHD or not, is extremely helpful.

is for Executive Functioning

Did you know?

- ADHD has been referred to as a 'disorder of self-regulation' due to impairment of executive functions (Barkley, 2011).

- Children with ADHD have a developmental delay in executive functioning skills by approximately 30 per cent or three to six years in comparison to their peers, meaning they have difficulty dealing with age-appropriate situations (ADHD Australia, 2019).

- Adults with ADHD tend to only develop approximately 75–80 per cent of the executive functioning capacity of their peers (which are usually fully developed by age 30), and so continue to lag being indefinitely (ADHD Australia, 2019).

ADHD is related to an atypical balance of brain chemicals in the prefrontal cortex part of our brains, which is responsible for our 'executive functioning'. Essentially, this means our decision making and self-regulation is likely to be impaired by ADHD, including the way we think things through, prioritise, manage our time and behave towards our future goals.

This can mean that some parts of our brain aren't as developed as other parts, and particularly in contrast to other people our age. Growing up, it always felt like I was somehow behind everybody else who understood what to do, as though they'd read a manual to life that I hadn't!

I think of it as the teacher in a classroom, except, for me, the teacher has been tied up in the corner of the room by the kids. It often feels like a committee of toddlers are in charge of my brain, pushing random buttons and doing whatever they want. It can often feel impossible to make them all work together.

The teacher might be screaming, but is ignored by the kids. This relates to our ability to know what we need to do but we *can't do it*. We might have all the tools and knowledge in the world, but if our brain isn't playing ball, we simply won't use them. The journals, self-help books, apps, voice-recording software and everything else will sit in the corner of the room along with the teacher, gathering dust.

This is why we can often think of ourselves as 'lazy, stupid and crazy' with ADHD (as inspired by a great book on ADHD called *You Mean I'm Not Lazy, Stupid or Crazy?!* by Kate Kelly and Peggy Ramundo). We might spend our lives thinking we're stupid because we can't do what everyone else is doing, lazy because we're not 'trying hard enough', or crazy because we're as surprised by our strong emotions as the people around us.

Crucially, the proven impairment of our prefrontal cortex demonstrates this is all false. *It is not our fault.* It's not our fault that we're not 'normal' (whatever normal means!) – there is a neurodevelopmental impact in our brains that prevents us from being able to do things, even those we might desperately want to do.

How is executive function affected by ADHD?

Executive function can be thought of in terms of the qualities described below, which can be seriously impaired by ADHD. As you read them, I suggest thinking about how these might have impacted you throughout your life, and how it feels to understand that these effects are literally just the way your brain is wired.

As in 'W is for Weaknesses', this definitely isn't a bad thing, but it can be very challenging to live with executive dysfunction in a world where everybody else seems to be able to just 'do' things so easily. I like to think of this as our brains still being in the 'hunter' mode of evolution from centuries ago; they haven't yet adapted for a society filled with expectations to be able to regulate ourselves and fall into line.

For example, compare sitting in an office for eight hours and memorising speeches to hunting woolly mammoths and building fires, where qualities such as lack of inhibition may have come in very useful!

Self-awareness

As in 'Y is for Your Body', we can be very unaware of our own bodies and experiences. This can range from not realising I need the bathroom or working without a break for hours on end when hyper-focused, to being unaware of how I feel in different situations.

Many of my ADHD coaching clients struggle with this in terms of being able to understand how their medication is impacting them, for example. If we're not conscious of how we feel 'normally', it can be difficult to notice any differences and use the benefits! Journaling or 'checking in with ourselves', as in 'G is for Grounding', can be very helpful to manage this.

Inhibition

This means our ability to restrain and control ourselves in different situations, which can be very problematic if we also can't control our emotions! For example, I was once very rude to someone I didn't know because they were being loud in a communal area before I even realised what I was doing, which I was absolutely mortified about afterwards.

As in 'I is for Impulsivity' and 'V is for Vices', a lack of inhibition can cause serious problems in making us vulnerable to exploitation and dangerous decisions. Whilst it can be great in making us very brave, there's real value in being able to choose when we use this quality!

Non-verbal working memory

This is the ability to hold things our mind, and picture things mentally. Our memory is significantly impacted by ADHD, such as forgetting people's names as soon we're told them or forgetting appointments and even entire events. For example, I really struggle to remember my childhood and certain events that happened throughout my life.

An impaired memory makes it very difficult to organise, start and focus on tasks, because we might forget what we're meant to be doing many times along the way. Whilst other people may be able to easily draw on their past experiences and lessons learned, we might easily forget our past and repeat mistakes several times over!

Visual reminders such as whiteboards are really important to balance this out, as we struggle to picture things in our mind.

Verbal working memory

This is our inner monologue or internal speech. As a child, I was obsessed with trying to turn off the constant buzz of thoughts blaring in my brain, which sounds like white noise. For me, I learned that writing things out helped me to process my thoughts, which is how I've managed to write books along the way! This book started as me trying to process my own thoughts about my ADHD.

For ADHD-ers, our inner monologues can be stuck on very negative channels, as in 'K is for Kindness'. Years of trying to fit into a neurotypical world can lead us to subconsciously be our own worst critics. It was incredibly empowering for me to learn how to tune in to this inner radio channel and to realise that my thoughts weren't real – and I could change the station if I wanted.

Meditation can be very helpful for this, as can other activities such as exercise, as in 'Z is for Zen'.

Emotional self-regulation

Whilst most people can use their executive functioning skills to control their emotions and process their feelings, people with ADHD may find this very difficult. As a result, our emotions can feel like gigantic tidal waves hitting us without warning, destroying everything in our path.

Whenever I'm stressed, my ADHD symptoms become much worse, which makes me more stressed! It's normal for us all to experience a spectrum of emotions, but with ADHD, these can filter over into other areas of our life, such as work or personal relationships that have nothing to do with the cause of our emotions. The positive is that we're able to feel things very deeply, including emotions such as excitement or happiness.

However, we might also have times of being unaware of our own feelings to the point that they explode in one go, which often happens to me. This can be quite scary to experience, especially if it's anger, as it seemingly comes out of nowhere. It's also led to me being called a 'drama queen' and 'attention seeker' throughout my life, which only made everything worse!

Self-motivation

Having ADHD means we can really struggle with motivating ourselves to do things, especially when there's no immediate external consequence. This is essentially where we have to trick our brains into doing the things we don't want to do, like eating healthy food or exercising.

Combined with our struggles with time management, we may see zero point in doing things with no quick reward, such as saving money for our future. The secret to overcoming this is finding a way to artificially activate our motivation, such as by setting ourselves a shorter deadline or reward, or making something more exciting or scary.

Essentially, we're very good at sprints, but not so good at marathons – so we need to turn things into sprints!

Planning and problem-solving

In combination with the above, having ADHD means we can

really struggle to think through problems and how to solve them, because this requires imagining ourselves in the future. We might have trouble considering different options and consciously visualising what these might look like.

This means we solve problems differently to other people, which tends to be a good thing due to cognitive diversity! However, in combination with the above, such as challenges in emotional regulation, it can also lead to us becoming extremely overwhelmed by different problems. For example, I've spent a lot of time crying hysterically on the phone to the tax department, trying to figure out how to fill in the forms properly, which turned out to be very simple!

This is why people with ADHD might be excellent in some areas, especially ones that might seem challenging for neurotypical people, such as writing a book (or three!), but struggle significantly in other areas that might seem 'easy' to many people. I'd often spend hours agonising over very simple Excel sheets at work, despite being able to do an impossibly huge amount of work in very short time periods otherwise!

To overcome this, it can be helpful to understand our brains and what sorts of problems we find challenging, and to seek out support for this.

Taking control of our executive function

Although our ability to consciously manage ourselves is impacted by ADHD, this doesn't mean we *can't*. There are many objectively 'successful' ADHD-ers, such as Zooey Deschanel (2011), who would've had to learn, memorise and perform a *lot* of scripts for *New Girl*!

As an ADHD coach, I often work with people on challenges relating to their executive functioning by supporting them in the following ways:

Understanding our brains

It can be very helpful to consciously spend time thinking through our options and how our brains are naturally set up, instead of trying to force them to be different. I sometimes think of this as being an investigator, piecing chunks of a personality together to figure out what we need to do to motivate or organise ourselves, for example!

We do this by identifying a person's character strengths (such as creativity or social intelligence), their values (what qualities are important to them personally, such as financial security or justice), and identifying sources of potential motivation and purpose. When we've got a clear idea of what drives us more generally, we can draw on this as motivation.

There may also be certain ways that people process information better than others, such as by walking around whilst talking, listening to music whilst reading, or fidgeting whilst listening. It can be very helpful to identify what works for you so that you can find ways of implementing this when you need to, such as by having fidget toys to hand.

Prioritising goals

By taking the time to consciously think through the different things you want to do in line with the information relevant to yourself as above, it's easier to identify what might be 'urgent', 'important' or 'not urgent or important'.

A question I often ask myself is 'How much will this matter in three days, three weeks, or three months?' This can help me think about things in perspective, and to realise I have a lot more time than I think – it doesn't all need to get done today!

Breaking things down into chunks

As we can really struggle with prioritising information, this can lead us to becoming too overwhelmed to make any decisions at all. A good approach is to identify just *one* goal in any situation such as this, just as a first step.

When thinking of something you want to do, try to identify one tiny step you can take, just to get started. You don't need to see the whole staircase, but just the step in front of you.

Externalising information

As our brains struggle with working memory and visualising information, it can be incredibly useful to externalise information we want to process or remember. For example, clients of mine have made vision boards, set up post-it notes around their homes, used journals, calendars and whiteboards to set themselves visual reminders.

I've had signs on my door reminding me to check for my keys or turn my straighteners off, sticky notes on my coffee machine instructing me to meditate for five minutes first, and white boards spelling out what I'm doing each day. It can also be really helpful to ask other people to do this for you, such as asking a manager to write down instructions or feedback for you to process properly, as we might not be able to retain or understand everything during a conversation. This is especially important if it's an emotionally charged situation, such as a performance review, which might make us feel anxious.

In our modern world, it might feel tempting to use apps to externalise information, but I'd recommend being careful to only use one or two apps at a time. This is speaking from experience of downloading lots of different apps and becoming even more overwhelmed! It is a really good idea to store all of your personal information somewhere secure, such as a programme that can hold your passwords, to ensure that you have all of these in one place.

Figuring out routines and processes

When we have a strong understanding of ourselves, we can order the things we need to do each day in advance to do the thing we don't want to do first! This avoids us having it looming over our day.

For example, if I don't exercise first thing in the morning, it's very unlikely that I will actually do it in the day. This can also be applied to situations such as work, in creating firm boundaries for our working hours, and actively planning in breaks for us to ensure we don't burn out.

This can be helpful to do by yourself first thing in the morning, such as by using a planner with the day broken into hourly chunks. We can also plan out processes with mini rewards, such as figuring out what we *want* to do (such as go on social media) and telling ourselves we can do this after doing something we *don't* want to do (such as finishing a report).

It can also be very helpful to think of your day in chunks, as in 'T is for Time Management', such as by using a pomodoro timer[1] to give yourself dedicated focus times, with only one task for each period of time.

Having accountability

We can also externalise the literal thinking parts of our brains to other people. For example, the UK Government can fund a support worker via Access to Work, which has been a lifesaver for me in being self-employed. This person supports me in doing my work, such as by organising appointments, and keeping me updated on what my priorities should be each day.

This is slightly more intensive than an ADHD coach, which Access to Work also funded alongside the support worker. The coach helps with the things I'm writing about here, enabling me to figure out the best processes and ways of motivating me, and the support worker helps ensure these things happen as they should.

However, you can also ask friends or family members for help with this. Just having one other person to help you make decisions (especially small ones, which can feel frustratingly overwhelming, such as what to eat for dinner!), or to be aware of what you're doing each day, can be very helpful. There are dedicated websites which can link you up to another person as an accountability buddy,[2] also referred to as a Body Double, and you both say what you're going to work on and do this alongside each other.

I had one client who came to me not being able to clean her

---

1   https://pomofocus.io
2   For example, www.iampayingattention.co.uk

house for years, and within just one week, she'd completed her five-week goals of completely transforming her house. She managed to do this by sending me photos of the house, and said she was so mortified at showing a stranger the photos that she had no choice but to clean it all up!

Mindfulness and therapy

To understand and manage our emotions, it can be very helpful to work with a therapist. Observing our own patterns, mood swings and triggers can help us to regulate our emotions. For example, if we know we'll be in a highly stressful situation, then we can take action around this to ensure we're as supported as possible, particularly in relation to our executive functioning, such as by giving ourselves a break from work.

Mindfulness, as in 'Z is for Zen', can also be very useful for this. Although we might have trouble sitting still and meditating (as per this chapter!), there are various activities we can do to simply notice our own inner experiences and focus on our breath. This might include exercise or journaling, for example.

Executive functioning can be an overwhelming thing to learn about (even the concept itself can feel quite abstract), but, ultimately, it just relates to how our brains are wired. We're likely to be adventurous, brave, creative, passionate and authentically ourselves, but it's very helpful to learn how to adapt our brains to get the most out of our lives here in this modern society!

F

is for Finance

Did you know?

- Studies have shown that individuals with more severe ADHD symptoms during childhood have more difficulty paying bills and are more likely to be in debt as adults, have less savings and be more likely to delay buying necessities (Liao, 2o2o). It was suggested that medication can mitigate these problems.

- Adults with ADHD are far more likely than those without to engage in risky financial behaviour, such as taking out expensive loans or making impulsive purchases without thinking the implications through fully (Meijer, 2o19).

- Saving money can be very hard for people with ADHD (Meijer, 2o19), as it is difficult to plan for the future or think about things in the long term, as in 'T is for Time Management'.

- ADHD is thought to cost approximately £16oo per year per person in money management fees (Jones, 2o22).

Having ADHD can be expensive. The combination of acting on impulsive thoughts, inattention to detail and lust for adrenaline can result in many expensive decisions that can keep you looped into an addictive cycle – feeling guilty for purchases and buying yourself more to feel better. This isn't even to mention the fact that people who have ADHD can struggle with holding down jobs and earning a stable income.

If you're in the UK, and your ADHD amounts to a disability protected by the Equality Act 2010[1] (i.e., it has a 'substantial' and 'long-term' negative impact on your ability to do normal daily activities), you may be entitled to government support. You wouldn't necessarily be told this after having a medical assessment, as it'd typically be dependent on the context being considered. However, seeing as an ADHD diagnosis requires at least two areas of your life to be negatively impacted over a long period of time, it's likely to be a strong contender![2]

Financial support from the government could include things such as Access to Work, as in 'J is for Jobs', which can provide funding for measures that can help you stay in employment (including self-employment), such as a job coach, support worker or special equipment. There is a range of potential benefits that can help, so definitely do your research in understanding where and how you can be supported – the UK Government lists these online.[3]

Saving arguably doesn't come naturally to any of us, let alone people who have ADHD. Things like tax, numbers and budgeting can seem complicated and detail-oriented – we tend to live in the now, which can make life difficult in the future. For example, if you are self-employed, then you will need to put aside a portion of your income each month to save for a tax payment at the end of the year. If you have a

---

1   www.gov.uk/definition-of-disability-under-equality-act-2010
2   As a person under the age of 18, the requirements include displaying symptoms for at least six months, with symptoms starting before age 12, in two different settings, such as home and school, which make your life considerably more difficult, and which are not part of a 'difficult phase'. See www.nhs.uk/conditions/attention-deficit-hyperactivity-disorder-adhd/diagnosis.
3   www.gov.uk/financial-help-disabled

rental agreement, you may need to make sure that you have enough income each month to be able to afford the rent. If you have an overdraft, this can often seem like free money – especially if you have difficulties keeping up with the logistics (such as remembering all of the different passwords – see 'O is for Organisation') to keep track of what you are spending.

Luckily, there are many different ways of making managing finances easier these days. Mobile banking apps such as Monzo and Starling allow you to 'lock away' certain amounts of money each month in pots which cannot be accessed. They can also notify you every time you spend money, which is a great reminder of how much you are spending. As we become more of a cashless society with online spending, it has become easier than ever to spend money without realising. I have found online banking is a very helpful way to keep track of my outgoing payments. I am able to review these regularly and properly appreciate how I am spending my money. You could also choose not to have an overdraft option, which prevents the risk of falling into debt. It's worth speaking to any service providers that you make regular payments to and asking whether you can set similar 'spending limits' – I have one with my phone provider which means I never need to worry about accidentally racking up huge bills!

For people who are self-employed, a programme called QuickBooks has allowed me to manage my accounting, invoices and taxes in an organised way for the first time ever! I also strongly recommend an app called Your Juno, which is a brilliant financial empowerment and educational app, making complicated terms very easy to understand.

When it comes to finance, everyone is in a different financial situation and will manage their money differently. Some people have unhealthy habits in relation to online shopping, others to gambling or signing up to new memberships that can easily be forgotten about. It's helpful to identify any patterns of problems you might be encountering. Unfortunately, the world we live in has made it easier than ever for us to fritter away money mindlessly. The 'subscription era' is not well suited to the impulsive nature of ADHD, as free trials and seemingly small purchases can quickly add up to large chunks of money.

Subscriptions are designed to make it hard to quit. When you sign up to a free trial, you will often have to cancel within a certain period; otherwise, the subscription will auto-renew. The cancelling process can be quite bureaucratic and difficult, having to go on to different pages, remember various passwords, and speak to a range of people. It requires sustained mental effort on something that is fairly boring and can seem pointless when it is a 'small' cost.

If you are anything like me, you will also have signed up to a fair few of these free trials with different email addresses and passwords. Trying to figure out all of the accounts and passwords can feel like banging your head against a brick wall – but it is worth it.

Here are some golden rules I have to follow to help me with my finances:

→ **Avoid subscriptions and free trials.** If you *must*, then write down your accounts and passwords in a designated (hidden!) journal or using a password-protector programme such as LastPass – see 'O is for Organisation' for more. Set yourself reminders of when these renew on your phone a few days in advance and make sure you cancel them, if you want to.

→ **Avoid websites that make it very easy to purchase things.**
I noticed a thought pattern developing in me where I
would literally wake up and think of things that I needed
to buy, buy them and forget. I loved the dopamine high
of coming home to presents I forgot that I'd ordered – but
not the huge amount of money it involved. This includes
websites that sell everything you could possibly think of,
which result in seconds between having the thought and
purchase. Block them off your phone if you have to – I do!

→ **Avoid debt!** If you are in debt, consider options such as
talking to charities that can support you or organisations
such as Debtors Anonymous, and make a plan to get out
of it as soon as you can. Try to avoid any forms of debt,
even if it doesn't seem like debt in the form of taking out a
loan – such as 'late payment' options or buying products
on 'credit' and signing up to contracts where you pay them
back over the long term. These can quickly spiral out of
control and it's very difficult to keep track of the different
interest rates that you might be being charged.

→ **Try to avoid free shipping.** It might not seem to make
sense in intentionally setting yourself a higher cost to
purchase something, but that one thought process of 'Oh
this shipping will cost me £3.50. Do I *really* need this?'
is important. It's essentially trying to make as many of
these types of 'Do I need it?' thoughts as possible. For me,
accounts with free next-day shipping tend to be the worst
for my impulsive buys, so I avoid signing up to 'cheap'
monthly memberships which offer these.

→ **Keep the bulk of your money in one or two savings
accounts.** These should be difficult to access, with standing
monthly payments arranged to come from these, such as

bills. Designate one bank account for 'spending', where you can pay yourself a budget each month. Try to avoid any overdraft options and, if possible, arrange to be notified every time you spend money.

→ **Try to avoid having your bank card enabled for spending on your phone.** The idea is to make it as hard as possible for you to spend money – so you have to actually get your card out of your pocket before spending money on something you might not need. Cash could also be a good option (though I tend to spend all of it whenever I have some!) – know yourself and what works best for you in terms of delaying the time between 'I want to buy that' and actually buying it.

→ **Avoid buying things that have free returns.** We want to reduce the bureaucracy involved *after* a purchase but increase the bureaucracy *before* one. I can find it really tough going to the post office and the processes involved to return a purchase make it so difficult that I end up keeping it.

→ **Avoid spending money on apps.** These are designed to be easy to purchase and difficult to cancel – and it can be hard to keep track of what you do and do not use.

→ **Notice if other people expect you to spend money on them.** As ADHD-ers tend to detest details and be susceptible to people-pleasing, others around you may be used to you picking up the dinner bill when it is too much faff to split it individually or to follow up afterwards to ask to be repaid. Make a conscious effort to not spend money on anybody but yourself for a while and to avoid taking the role of 'pay me back later'.

→ **Be mindful about your spending.** By keeping a spending diary and physically asking yourself before each purchase if something is absolutely necessary, you can keep track of how you spend your own money.

→ **Keep a 'virtual shop' in a diary.** When you want to buy something, write it down in a notebook. This will satisfy the part of your brain that wants to feel like it's 'acted' upon the thought, and if you can, dedicate a specific 'buying' time of the week or month to look at the notebook and potentially act upon it. I often find that I don't actually want the things even a day later!

How to make a budgeting plan

Do a mindful financial self-assessment

Print out your most recent bank statement. Go through it and write out every recent purchase and whether it was necessary or not and try to identify the thinking behind it. Notice if it was useful looking back, and whether you regret purchasing it. Try to identify patterns in your spending, and simply notice how it feels. Ideally for a week, but even for one day, write down every time you want to purchase something and the reasons behind it. Try to catch yourself and notice *why* you want to buy something and whether it is really necessary.

Identify your income and necessary expenses each month

These are the outgoing costs that are necessary for your survival. They include electricity, water, rent and groceries – the bare minimum that you need to get by. Observe these two total figures and look at what you have when you subtract the necessary costs from your income. This is your spending money for the month.

Make a clean start

Identify any 'unnecessary' subscriptions that come out of your account each month and cancel them. See if you can live without them for a month. Make yourself commit to sitting for 25 minutes at a time and cancelling your subscriptions. If you find that you want them after a month, you can return, but give yourself a break and make a fresh start from zero. This counts even for yearly subscriptions – make the effort to cancel all of them in one go.

Choose how you want to spend and save your money

It's helpful to use an app like Monzo where you can put a specific amount of spending money aside each month. There are ways that you can put half of the money in a pot that is unlocked halfway through the month or saving pots that you can only access on certain dates. Simplify your spending and saving to the bare minimum of bank accounts – a saving and spending account.

If you want to start saving money, start small. Even just £10 per month can make a difference – that is £120 per year, the equivalent of two coffees a month. Choose a small amount to save each month and stick to it. You can always increase it in the future, but don't start with trying to save hundreds and failing straight away. Learn the art of slow saving.

With your remaining money, choose what you want to do with it. Do you want to split it into two sections? Do you tend to spend a lot at the start of the month? What are your weaknesses? Make a plan of how you want to spend your money and on what – this could be experiences, a holiday or clothes – but whatever it is, make sure that you actively choose it.

Make a blockage plan

Your bank account will show your weaknesses. If there is something you want to stop spending money on, such as clothes from a particular online shop, or eating out, make a plan to focus on making this as hard as possible for yourself. This could involve blocking certain websites from your browser, deleting certain apps from your phone, limiting yourself to one restaurant meal per week, taking lunch into work with you – whatever it is, you know how to target it. Start small and build up slowly.

For example, if you buy lunch every single day of the week, resolve to take in a lunch for just one day. Knowing that you *can* do it if you want to is the first step towards breaking these habits.

Check in at the end of the week

Set yourself a reminder on your phone to check your bank account at a time when you know you will have ten minutes to look at it. Review your spending each week and notice any differences in your finances overall. Remember not to beat yourself up if you still have an impulsive spend, but just to acknowledge it. If you can, find an accountability buddy to go through your spending each weekend with.

is for Grounding

Did you know?

- It is estimated that one in four people in prison may have ADHD (Campbell, 2022), though in many cases this may not be formally recognised. A Swedish study found that people with ADHD are more likely to commit crimes (37% of men and 15% of women) than those without it (9% of men and 2% of women). Medication was proven to reduce this (Karolinska Institutet, 2012).

- Adults with ADHD are nine times more likely to end up in prison than those of a similar age and background who do not have ADHD. They also experience more financial instability and are more likely to have been fired from a job (Born to Be ADHD, 2017).

- Mindfulness meditation has been found to be effective in treating adults with ADHD, following a study in 2017 (Mitchell *et al.*, 2017). This has been equated with focusing one's attention on the present moment with 'purpose', then approaching that moment with open-mindedness.

ADHD-ers tend to be filled with ideas and move very quickly through life, which is a brilliant thing, but it can also mean being almost too busy to actually be present and 'live' fully, or to think things through.

It can be very difficult to ground yourself and to enforce some stability into your life when everything is so fast-moving and exhilarating. I used to dread the idea of a routine and knowing what I will be doing each day, thinking this would make for a predictable, boring life. However, this predictability is what allows us to feel secure enough to live our lives to the fullest. As in 'I is for Impulsivity', routines can feed into our overall structure underpinning a stable, yet exciting, life.

Anxiety is commonly linked to ADHD. We can be crippled with worry over seemingly easy tasks, such as administration and cleaning, which can feel very overwhelming, combined with beating ourselves up for not being able to do them. In contrast, daring activities such as bungee jumping or moving to a new country can seem comparatively easy – we tend to be good in a crisis because of the adrenaline that stimulates our brains. Contrastingly, the small things that most people do on autopilot can easily all pile up into one insurmountable chore-mountain of stress for us.

This is where grounding steps in. Having a routine allows you to train yourself to do these small tasks on autopilot mode. It is training yourself to do these small tasks easily. It allows you to know what to expect and to stop worrying about it all – the framework for your life is in place.

There are a variety of ways that you can ground yourself, and each person will be different in what helps them feel secure and stable.

Finding a routine

A routine is a sequence of actions regularly followed. The point is to find the *right* routine for you, that helps you feel grounded and secure. Something that does not change, no matter where you are in the world or what is happening in your life. Think of having a routine as the scaffolding around you as a human being, the structure that keeps you steady and upright.

There are many different ways of finding a healthy routine, which will depend on the person. Above all, it needs to be *realistically achievable and sustainable*. A morning routine is a good place to start, with an additional evening routine as an ideal end goal.

Think about what your morning currently looks like. How long do you have between waking up and leaving the house? Do you feel stressed out in the mornings, or forget things? What could you add in to make things a little more peaceful for yourself?

Ideas for a morning routine could include:

→ waking up half an hour earlier

→ meditating

→ drinking a glass of water or hot drink as soon as you wake up

→ waking up at the same time every day

→ doing exercise, such as yoga or going for a run

→ writing in a journal

→ having the same breakfast every day

→ making your bed.

I would advise trying to incorporate a morning routine that you do *before* looking at your phone – where it is very easy to fall into a scrolling vortex! The problem with our phone is that it tends to rule us, rather than the other way around, as it has been designed by experts to be as addictive as possible. Even if we go on to look at one thing, our attention tends to become side-tracked by things we may not have intended to start our day with, such as negative news or social media.

→ Try to limit your phone usage in the mornings in particular – remember that how you start your day sets the tone for the rest of it. One idea to limit phone usage in the mornings is to charge it in a different room to the one you sleep in – and invest in an alarm clock!

→ As we will see in 'O is for Organisation', there are also things that you can incorporate into your morning routine that will make your life easier for the rest of the day. For example, you could have a list on your door of all the things you need to remember before leaving (such as keys, wallet, turning the heaters off…) or write a to-do list first thing in the morning. Whiteboards tend to be great for this, as you can clearly plan out your priorities for the day.

→ It is also helpful to have an evening routine, because people who have ADHD often suffer with sleep problems, as in 'S is for Sleep'. An evening routine can signal to your brain that it is ready to switch off and relax, setting you up for a good night's sleep. If we end our day on our phones, it's likely to keep our brains in the alert, restless mode that is not conducive to rest.

Activities that an evening routine could involve include:

→ switching off any technology one hour before going to sleep

→ having an allocated 'bedtime' each night

→ meditating

→ yoga or another form of exercise

→ drinking a non-caffeinated drink at a certain time

→ eating dinner at a certain time

→ writing in a journal – gratitude diaries are particularly helpful

→ cleaning your room

→ reading.

Think about what your ideal morning and evening routine would look like. Now, pick *one* of those things, for one time of day. To make a routine, it is important that it is realistic for you to do over a long period of time to form a habit, rather than a grand routine that you will be able to stick to for a few days before feeling bad about forgetting to do it and giving up.

Write down the one thing that you would like to incorporate into your routine to start with, along with the exact time and length of time that you will be doing it for – make sure it is so small that it doesn't seem worth doing. For example, you may write down, 'Meditate for one minute each morning'.

This tiny change will grow as you do it. If you can allow yourself to simply stick with one small task each day for a month, it will become a habit and prove to you that you *can* commit to a routine. You can then incorporate another task or make it longer. The idea is to grow your routine over time and make it part of your framework. Watch out for anything that could be a potential blockage to your routine – for example, using an app on your phone to meditate. This will necessarily involve using your phone and mean that you waste time scrolling rather than meditating.

Grounding activities

It can be very useful to identify a hobby or activity that you can do to feel calm and connect to yourself. For example, I really love doing yoga and rollerblading, and know that if I'm feeling down, these things will help me to improve my mood.

This could also include things such as cooking yourself food, calling somebody you care about or having a massage. It might be helpful to put these down in a list that you can easily access when feeling overwhelmed.

Returning to these basic activities that make us feel happy can ground us wherever we are in the world, bringing us home to ourselves. They can get us out of our minds and into our bodies and empower us to consciously regulate our own emotions.

Finding an anchor

Think of your ADHD-mind as a helium-filled balloon. An anchor can be thought of as something or someone who will hold your balloon down to the floor, so you don't fly off and pop in the sky. I have found it particularly helpful to ground myself by having a dedicated person or 'thing' in my life to ground me.

It's finding something to commit to that you care about deeply, that you cannot easily give up and which will not give up on you, when the going gets tough. Having an anchor helps us remember why we are doing it in the first place, and to work through any difficulties.

Examples of anchors could be our best friends, therapists, pets, family and so on. They are the things that we have to put in effort for, such as waking up early to walk a dog on cold, dark mornings, but we do it because we ultimately love them – which does not change when things become stressful.

Before I was diagnosed with ADHD, I often felt like a balloon that could float away at any point. Without any clear anchors, I found myself spontaneously making important life choices such as moving country, because I didn't feel like I belonged anywhere.

These days, I can notice these impulsive, often catastrophic, thoughts pop into my head, but I can calm them down by reminding myself of my anchors. For me, these are the people in my life that care about me, such as my family and friends, my work, especially my coaching clients, and my support system of professionals, such as my coach and doctor.

As well as enabling me to feel as though I have purpose and belonging, these anchors remind me to prioritise my own self-care. I can't give from an empty cup, so I have to ensure I'm looking after myself in order to be able to show up for the people in my life, as in 'L is for Love'.

It can be helpful to keep a reminder of these anchors close by, such as having framed photographs of your loved ones on display. As ADHD-ers can experience difficulties with 'object permanence', where we struggle to think of things when we're not actively around them, this can be a really useful way to remind ourselves of all of the wonderful ways we belong.

is for Hyper-Focus

Did you know?

- ADHD has been scientifically linked to the ability to 'hyper-focus' (Hupfeld, Abagis & Shah, 2019). This means episodes of long-lasting, highly focused attention, which suggests that ADHD doesn't necessarily mean there is an attention 'deficit', but an unique way of paying attention.

- People with ADHD may 'mask' their symptoms by working extremely hard to imitate others, which can result in misdiagnosis.

- It has been proven that adults with ADHD may succeed professionally despite significant symptoms of inattention and executive dysfunction (Palmini, 2008). They may be less likely to seek help, but have incredibly low self-esteem and overcompensate in ways that could result in burnout.

My ability to hyper-focus is both my favourite and least- favourite part about having ADHD. It's amazing to be able to pick up an entire subject in a week and to learn so much about the world, but incredibly frustrating when the interest passes and you're on to the next thing. It also leads to indecision in other areas of your life, such as trying to choose a job or partner! It can make me feel like a huge imposter, such as learning my entire year of university law work in one month before my exams, despite not attending many lectures.

However, we all just have different ways of learning, and it's definitely not bad to have interests!

Hyper-focus refers to an intense fixation on an interest or activity for an extended period of time and is commonly associated with ADHD. It is similar to being in a state of 'flow', or 'in the zone' – where we're completely absorbed in what we're doing, as though we could stay doing it forever (Csikszentmihalyi & Csikszentmihalyi, 1988).

This can be great, but everything else in the world is blocked out to focus on this one thing – it's like the opposite of not being able to pay attention: not being able to stop paying attention, similar to binge-watching an addictive TV series. For example, I've had periods where I would wake up at 6am and work until 12am, hardly eating anything and not moving for the entire day – this is an extremely unhealthy way to live!

In one study on hyper-focus, a research participant described it as 'brain caviar...being able to channel all that random energy that's flying around in my head into one intense hyper-focused sort of beam...it's giving the brain a task that it's almost designed for'. They described the ADHD brain energy as being 'unfocused, quite scattered, chaotic and a bit random, but give that brain something that you can really tune into... I get this incredible intense concentration and that's great for work' (Miranda *et al.*, 2012, p.244).

This is quite ironic when ADHD stands for a 'deficit' of attention. It feels like the attention system of ADHD-ers is dysregulated rather than defective – if we want to focus on something, we might be able to do so much more effectively than a neurotypical person would be able to.

It's just that we don't always have much choice about what we want to focus on, and our brains refuse to focus on things we aren't interested in – wanting and choosing do not come from the same part of our brain. We can *want* to eat ice cream for breakfast, but we *choose* to eat cereal. So, whilst writing an entire book in a week might be achievable for someone with ADHD, tasks such as washing up or taking out the rubbish may be a completely different story.

Many people I've coached, particularly students, can also end up hyper-focusing on small details, which prevents them from getting the 'big things' done. For example, rewriting a paragraph of an essay for hours on end, instead of writing the whole essay! I try to remind myself that 'done is better than perfect', and to get out of my own hyper-focus when this happens to me. Hyper-focusing isn't always helpful!

Hyper-focus is thought to result from abnormally low levels of dopamine, which makes it difficult to 'shift gears' to do the boring but necessary tasks – or anything that isn't your focus of the moment. It can feel like having a superpower, but it can also feel exhausting and annoying – it needs to be regulated.

The trick is figuring out how to shift the gears and spread your hyper-focus across things equally, and how to trick yourself into *wanting* to do things that you don't really want to do. Once you understand your hyper-focus and what drives it, you can learn to train it, and apply the brakes!

This may require external stimulation, such as timers and alarm clocks. Calendars, to-do lists, written visual reminders and physical signals such as vibrating fitness watches are great ways of training yourself both to do a task you don't really want to do and to take breaks from hyper-focusing.

Think of yourself as a child who needs to be convinced into doing things they don't want to do, such as eating broccoli. You might disguise the broccoli as chips or play an airplane game with it or let the child watch TV afterwards if they eat it. It might seem silly to think of yourself in this way, but try to get in touch with your inner child that simply does not want to do the boring things – and watch your life change.

When you hyper-focus a lot, particularly if this is on your job (hello, fellow workaholics!), you might ironically appear as though you don't have ADHD, especially given the general stigma of it relating to people who can't focus at all. In truth, we might be able to hyper-focus on certain things that might appear challenging to neurotypical people but be completely unable to do 'easy' tasks like washing our clothes!

People have told me that I can't have ADHD because of my 'achievements' such as writing books. Ironically, the reality is that it's my ADHD that has caused me to become hooked on the adrenaline and dopamine highs of constantly working to unhealthy degrees, and I have to continuously work on trying to balance it; otherwise, I burn out.

This can also lead to us both feeling unable to ask for help and isolating ourselves in unhealthy working patterns, because we can get a whole month of work done in one day and feel frustrated at other people who (understandably) can't keep up. Being able to ask for and accept help is important in all areas of our life: we cannot do it all. It's not sustainable to live in a state of hyper-focus, and the crashes, as in 'B is for Burnout', can be debilitating.

As in the Disney movie *Soul*, hyper-focus can effectively cut us off from reality. This means that we miss out on all the wonderful things life has to offer and cut off our own feelings in the process. We can become 'human doings' instead of human beings.

'Y is for Your Body' talks about the sensory impacts of ADHD, which can become very apparent when you're hyper-focused. For example, not going to the bathroom for the whole day despite really needing to, because what you're doing is so important, or realising that you've been sitting in a hunched-up ball for seven hours! For me, hyper-focus is very mentally strenuous, and it almost feels like disconnecting from my body.

Hyper-focus itself can be a distraction to avoid feelings or things we don't want to do. Focusing on 'work' seems like a 'productive' procrastination – but can be difficult to explain to others who believe you're just not trying hard enough, as in 'L is for Love'.

It's like tidying your bedroom by shoving everything into your wardrobe and living in fear that somebody will open the wardrobe. Everything looks neat and tidy, until the wardrobe explodes.

It's a horrible feeling when the intense level of interest subsides, and we simply can't pay attention anymore, because our brains are obsessing over something else. However, there's almost nothing better than the feeling of having our interest sparked by something and embarking upon the journey of learning *everything* about it, *right now.*

Hyper-focus gives us the keys to our attention-span: by training it, we can use this ability to laser-focus to do brilliant things, like writing a book about ADHD!

How to train your hyper-focus

1. Try to think of a time that you have hyper-focused on something in your life. This could be anything from a project you were particularly interested in to a book that you couldn't put down.

   > For example, I hyper-focused when writing *The Model Manifesto*, waking up at 6am and writing non-stop until I went to sleep.

2. Write down the reasons why you were hyper-focused, what made you interested on that occasion – your 'hyper-focus triggers'. What was it about the situation that you were particularly interested in? People with ADHD tend to react to novelty, external stimulation (such as deadlines) and excitement.

   > I was hyper-focused because I was extremely passionate about helping other models avoid exploitation, and writing often makes me lose track of time. I also had a short deadline and a lot of fear about the external reactions to the book, so I wanted to make sure it was perfect. It was also pretty exciting!

3. Try to identify the feelings you had when you were hyper-focusing. What did you miss out on whilst hyper-focusing – what were the negatives associated with it? What typically happens after a period of hyper-focusing?

   > I felt passionate about the book but nothing else, meaning I

> missed out on a few months of my life. I became so obsessed with the book that it took over everything, making me avoid seeing friends or family at all. I became very stressed out and lost a huge amount of weight, missing meals, not exercising, and feeling depressed by the end of it, because I felt quite numb and terrified about what would come next!

4. Write down three ways that you can manage your hyper-focus when it next occurs, such as designating breaks by setting alarms or making a sustainable plan, as in 'T for Time Management'.

> Break down and plan my work in advance in a calendar, allotting one to two hours at a time to each task. Set myself alarms and reminders after each designated time period. Intentionally give myself much longer than I think I'll need as a deadline (and tell other people this!).

5. Write down three things that you wish you could hyper-focus on, such as cleaning. Now, find a way of applying your 'hyper-focus triggers' to these activities – you may have to use your imagination! For example, you could think of a game to clean as much as possible in five-minute bursts to your favourite songs.

> Cooking: dedicate some time on the weekend to listening to a podcast on a topic I'm passionate about, whilst cooking a big meal.
>
> Cleaning: play my favourite song every morning and clean as much as I can with the deadline of a few minutes!
>
> Exercise: join a sports team for the extra accountability of other people, which will make me want to show up consistently and be more exciting.

Tips

▸ Use calendars, alarm clocks and vibrating watches to remind yourself to take a break throughout the day, incorporating this into your routine.

▸ Try to incorporate a routine of exercise each day. This will help you get out of your mind and into your body!

▸ When you feel that you are becoming hyper-focused on something, tell someone you trust. As in 'B is for Burnout', the goal is having an accountability buddy to help you avoid the crash!

▸ Remember that it's completely fine to be interested in lots of different things, and then not to be. A book called *Refuse to Choose*, by Barbara Sher, is brilliant for this.

▸ Break tasks down into tiny steps. Try to make an effort to set realistic deadlines, with more time than you think you need, and to take things slowly.

▸ Make sure that you have eight hours of sleep per night. As in 'S is for Sleep', this is very important for managing ADHD symptoms. Turn off any electronic devices an hour before going to sleep and charge them in a different room.

▸ Try to separate your work and personal life. Set yourself the latest time you want to be at work, say 7pm, and make sure that you leave. Try to disconnect your work emails from your phone and establish a boundary between the two worlds.

▶ Remember that being diagnosed with ADHD, taking medication or receiving any kind of help in managing your ADHD symptoms will not negatively impact your ability to hyper-focus. It will actually make you *more* productive, as you can choose to channel your energy in a sustainable, effective way – and enjoy your life!

is for Impulsivity

Did you know?

- The part of our brain that sends signals to allow or stop behaviour (the 'thalamus gate') is impacted by ADHD, meaning that we may struggle to make long-term decisions or control ourselves in the short term, for example, interrupting others (Rodden & Nigg, 2o2o).

- High novelty-seeking and low self-directedness have been scientifically associated with the personality of a person with ADHD (Perroud *et al.*, 2o16). This could explain why ADHD-ers may feel interested in a lot of new things but become bored easily and move on to something else. In turn, this can result in low self-esteem and feelings of failure, as in 'W is for Weaknesses'.

- Impulsivity is associated with addiction, with about 25 per cent of adults being treated for alcohol and substance abuse thought to have ADHD (Watson, 2o2o).

Impulsivity can be incredibly annoying. It can feel like having a three-year-old child in charge of my brain at times, making decisions that I look back on in disbelief. For about six years, my 'word of the year' was stability. I never seemed to be able to find it, just veering from one huge change to another, unable to even decide which country to live in, let alone what job to do. Impulsivity itself can become addictive, as we constantly chase new highs and avoid boredom. We seek out novelty, excitement and fun, which can be good if our choices are healthy, such as trying out painting classes, but also very bad if they are unhealthy, like gambling or drugs.

It can feed into every aspect of our lives, from people-pleasing ('N is for No'), to bad choices ('V is for Vices'), to difficulties prioritising and cycles of self-hate as we prop up our stories of being unable to commit to anything ('Q is for Quitting').

However, it can also be a great asset, and for me it now equates to trusting my gut, as I live a relatively stable, yet still very fun life!

Many neurotypical people will stay in lives that don't make them particularly happy, because they've 'done all the work to get there'. In contrast, people with ADHD may change course throughout their lives many times, because they are no longer happy. It can lead to an authentic, interesting life filled with adventures – but it's important to try to establish some structure for it to be sustainable.

We might make decisions that seem bizarre to other people, but as I outline in 'K is for Kindness', once we start becoming compassionate towards ourselves, this doesn't really matter. This compassion can underpin our 'structure' to ensure that we aren't making decisions that will hurt us in the long run.

As in 'Q is for Quitting', there is a big difference between impulsively quitting a job versus a hobby. The trick to establishing a base foundation is training the flag in your brain to recognise this and implement brakes when needed, to slow down the decision-making process.

Think of your foundational structure as a tree trunk, with impulsive decisions as the branches. By laying the foundations, we can have the time, money and freedom to make all the impulsive decisions we want.

The secret is building in brain-brakes: taking the time to think about decisions carefully before making them. Ultimately, this simply involves us thinking something through from different angles than the 'I want to do this right now' one – which can be very persuasive! It's opening up a little room in your brain to hold thoughts before they translate into words or actions, where you can consider them in more detail.

Building this is important to ultimately allow you to trust yourself. Being diagnosed with ADHD can be confronting, because we can second-guess all of our decisions with the new lens of 'impulsivity', but it's important to remember that we're still the same person, and ADHD is simply part of who we are. Having self-compassion for ourselves allows us to remember that it's okay to make imperfect decisions, but learn from them for next time – ADHD or not!

My experience

When I graduated from university, I couldn't decide what job to do, which led to many years of impulsive decisions. I started and stopped different jobs constantly, which became worse and worse the more it happened. I felt both as though I'd never be able to get a 'real' job, but also like finding and keeping a job was signing myself up to a lifelong prison sentence, keeping me stuck in paralysis.

As we can struggle with making decisions and prioritising information, we might look to other people for advice or examples of what to do. Personally, I was constantly asking Google for advice on 'what to do with my life' and following whatever popped up – whether that was booking flights across the world or applying to random jobs like MI5! I was always beating myself up because I felt like these decisions made no sense, but, in retrospect, they were just because I felt so lost.

After I was diagnosed with ADHD, I found compassion for myself and tried out a 'real' job in law for two and a half years, before becoming an ADHD coach, alongside publishing books and having lots of fun adventures on the side!

I have the same brain as before I was diagnosed, but now have much more understanding and compassion for myself, which ultimately means I trust myself much more to make my own decisions without over- or under-thinking them.

How to reduce impulsive decisions

Having a foundation for us to make decisions from enables us to balance spontaneity with structure, or, in other words, having fun within a stable foundation! This is a base of self-trust and compassion, where we're able to think without constantly second-guessing ourselves.

Make conscious decisions

When we come across situations that might spark our tendency to be impulsive, it's good if we can slow down enough to think about whether this is something we actually *want* to do. What level of commitment do we want to put in, and why? How will we feel about this in three weeks, three months and three years?

It's ideal if we try out new things with less long-term obligations, such as a gym with a monthly-rolling contract, rather than one with a fixed term for 12 months!

For example, when I started going to jiujitsu, I decided that I wanted to go every Saturday morning for fun, for as long as I enjoyed it. In comparison, when I joined a cheerleading club, I impulsively agreed to do the competitions at the end of the year, feeling like I was trapped doing something I didn't enjoy because of this!

A key part of this is reminding ourselves that we can try it for fun, and it doesn't have to be forever. This could apply to jobs too – we'll all probably have lots of different careers throughout our lifetimes!

On the flip side, it's good for us to consciously choose to commit to what we say yes to. This might mean saying no to other things. I have a checklist I try to sign off against big decisions, asking myself what saying yes to this thing would mean saying no to in other areas of my life, and how long I want to dedicate to it before deciding whether to make it more long term.

Plan ahead

With the benefit of understanding our tendency to make impulsive decisions and impairments on our executive functioning skills, we can plan effectively. I like to think of this as 'locking myself in' to decisions so that I can't quit, which might sound a bit counter-intuitive, but is often necessary for a mind that reacts quickly without always thinking out the long-term consequences!

This means being aware that something might go wrong and being prepared to reactively adapt to it. It can be very useful to think ahead about potential impulsivity-related challenges in particular situations, such as the tendency to drink too much if we're going out with friends or quitting our jobs if we have a bad day. By taking some pro-active steps to avoid making these impulsive decisions, such as avoiding alcohol or speaking to someone we trust before quitting a job, we can feel more confident in the moment.

This can also apply more generally. For example, if we have particular habits that create issues with impulsivity, such as spending too much money, or sending messages we might regret later on, we can decide to change this in the future by planning ahead. I don't have a contactless card set up on my phone, and send all emotionally charged messages to a friend, or myself, before sending them to the person!

The key thing is to remember not to beat ourselves up over it: each mistake is a lesson for next time!

Plan for fun

People with ADHD tend to hate being bored, and novelty can wear off quickly, which can lead us to make more impulsive decisions. By actively planning for impulsivity and fun in the decisions we do make, we can find other ways of novelty that are slightly healthier than spontaneously uprooting our entire lives.

This could apply to things such as starting a new job or

signing up to a new course. If we're prepared for it to stop being 'sparkly and new', we can seek other sources of novelty without leaving the entire thing and starting again completely. It's good to have a pot of money each month that you can spend guilt-free on new hobbies, such as a gym membership, life-drawing classes, festivals and holidays! As we thrive on things we're interested in, we can search for inspiration on the side of our pre-existing commitments.

This might be as simple as volunteering for a charity, reading new books or visiting a friend in a new city for the weekend.

Avoid 'manufactured' impulsivity

Technology can easily exploit our impulsivity, as in 'F is for Finance'. For people who are already vulnerable to making choices without thinking out the long-term consequences, an app that shows us exactly what we want to see, for hours on end, can feed this part of our brain. It can give us impulsivity on a plate, constantly refreshing the screen and showing us new videos of cute animals.

However, technology addiction also makes us susceptible to exploitation by targeted advertising, and scrolling probably isn't how we want to spend the majority of our days.

Things like gambling, alcohol and drugs, as in 'V is for Vices', can also feed our dopamine-hunting brains, but in an unhealthy way, causing addiction. They can influence our lives in ways we don't intend and make it harder to do the things we want to do, so it's important to try to pro-actively avoid unhealthily manufactured dopamine hits.

is for Jobs

Did you know?

- People with untreated ADHD are twice as likely to have been fired from a job as people without ADHD (Barkley, 1988).

- If ADHD impacts a person significantly in their daily life, it can be seen as a disability under the Equality Act 2010, meaning that employers have a duty to protect employees from discrimination and make reasonable adjustments for them to do their jobs where necessary. The UK Government may be able to help fund these adjustments, such as a job coach, through a scheme called Access to Work.

- Studies have shown that certain ADHD traits, such as hyper-focus, may benefit entrepreneurs (Wiklund, Patzelt & Dimov, 2016). Research has shown that ADHD-ers have outperformed people without ADHD by generating more creative ideas and being more likely to find a correct solution to a problem; they have been shown to be highly creative, divergent thinkers and excellent problem solvers (Born to Be ADHD, 2017).

ADHD-ers make excellent employees, because we tend to be passionate, determined, creative, quick-thinking and empathetic, *especially* when we're interested in something. However, finding and keeping a job can be very difficult for us, because if we're *not* interested in something, it can be very hard for us to sustain our attention – and all jobs have parts that are more interesting than others.

On the other end of the scale, doing something we *are* particularly interested in can lead to burnout, as in 'B is for Burnout'. This could result in a person with ADHD steamrolling into a company with lots of grand ideas, before steamrolling out again a few months later. Our ADHD qualities can make us capable of doing work unlike any other employees are able to, as in 'H is for Hyper-Focus', but this can come at a cost when those qualities are over-used – and we're not always in control of this! ADHD can also clash with the bureaucracy of organisations, given our aversion to details and administrative tasks. We may also have to work closely alongside others on a daily basis, which can be difficult for ADHD-ers who are hyper-sensitive to rejection and prone to emotional dysregulation. For example, reacting impulsively after a difficult conversation can result in leaving a job without thinking it through properly.

Environments such as open-plan offices may not always be the best working environments for a person with ADHD to thrive, with background chats and endless opportunities for us to become distracted. As in 'Y is for Your Body', ADHD can result in sensory issues such as a strong aversion to smells – which could lead to unexpected outbursts when these build up, such as when colleagues microwave their lunches!

This isn't even to mention the stress of finding a job in itself. Which is difficult enough for everyone, let alone those with ADHD who struggle with forms, processes and Rejection Sensitive Dysphoria. From the very start of the process, it can be a nightmare: should ADHD be disclosed as a disability on the application form? It is a minefield of bureaucracy and confidence-testers, which can seem never-ending.

Researchers have found ADHD-ers are more likely to be self-employed (Verheul *et al.*, 2016), which can work well with our creative and entrepreneurial traits. Entrepreneurs such as Virgin Airlines founder Sir Richard Branson are great examples of this, and I've coached extremely successful CEOs who dropped out of school before finishing their exams.

However, with a lack of self-esteem, confidence and self-regulation, we might experience challenges in not reaching our full potential, taking on too much or failing due to a lack of structure to support us. We might undersell ourselves, or avoid vitally important parts of running a business, such as accounts, because we simply can't process it. It's good to know that the UK Government's Access to Work scheme applies to self-employed people too – for example, it can fund support workers who can provide administrative services, or workplace strategy coaching.

The freedom of being self-employed should be weighed carefully against the stability and routine of having a full-time job – different options may suit different people. Understanding ourselves is the first step in figuring out what works best for us in terms of employment.

Good jobs for ADHD-ers

It might be difficult to figure out what kind of job to do if you have ADHD, because we have a tendency to want to do *everything*, but it's difficult to know what the 'reality' of a job is like without trying it out. As a rough guide, the below elements may be good to incorporate into your career:

→ **Passion:** As ADHD-ers are often motivated by our interests and emotions, it's good to find a job that you feel passionate about, that has a *purpose* behind it. Finding our 'why' means that we always have something to inspire us, even when things become difficult. Examples could include charity work, social work, teaching or working with animals – or whatever your passion is.

→ **Adrenaline:** The ADHD mind is often seeking stimulation, adrenaline and excitement – we tend to be good in a crisis. We can thrive in challenging, fast-paced jobs that are motivated by a highly intense external environment. Examples could include being a paramedic, fire-fighter, working in the police force, surgeon, stockbroker, skydiving instructor or barrister – the list is endless!

→ **Variety:** Jobs where every day is different will help prevent us from getting bored. For example, jobs where you meet new people every day, such as being a barista, retail work, client-facing work such as being a therapist or customer service, to name a few.

→ **Creativity:** ADHD has been linked to high creativity levels, and creativity tends to spark happiness! Examples could include being an actor, artist, dancer, writer, designer or musician.

→ **Problem-solving:** People with ADHD tend to be good at this, and it's good for our 'out of the box' thinking to be valued in our work. For example, being an IT specialist, working in technology, product design or as a consultant.

→ **Movement:** For ADHD-ers with a lot of energy, as in 'Y is for Your Body', physical jobs may suit us very well. These could include working as an athlete, fitness trainer, waiter or waitress, tour guide or hairdresser.

→ **Supportive cultures:** Having ADHD means we might be extremely good at certain aspects of our jobs, but struggle more with others. We may also have different needs, such as the ability to work flexible hours or locations, which it can be helpful to ask potential employers about. I strongly recommend looking at their resources on 'disability' or 'neurodiversity', or speaking to current employees about the culture of a workplace.

Talking about ADHD at work

Under the Equality Act 2010, you are disabled if you have a physical or mental impairment that has a 'substantial' and 'long-term' negative effect on your ability to do normal daily activities. For the purposes of this chapter, this essentially means that you should never be discriminated against or treated negatively because of your ADHD in the workplace, including when applying for a job. It also means you should be supported by an employer to be able to participate in your work as your colleagues are able to, which is referred to as 'reasonable adjustments'.

Talking to your employer about ADHD is a deeply personal decision and can be very stressful. It can feel embarrassing, especially given the stigma about ADHD, and the need to 'disclose' it as a 'disability'. Eighty-two per cent of respondents to an ADDitude survey said they had not asked for workplace accommodations, and more than half hadn't disclosed their ADHD to their employer (ADDitude, 2020). Each person will have to weigh up the pros and cons of their own individual situation.

To help with these challenges, I set up ADHD Works, which

supports people to harness ADHD in the workplace with coaching and training. Head to my website, www.leannemaskell.com to learn more about this.

ADHD might not always feel like a disability, but it definitely can be in certain situations. Just because it is invisible doesn't mean that it doesn't severely impact your life. If you're coming up against struggles that directly relate to your ADHD at work, I'd personally recommend talking about it to someone that you trust if you're able to, because you deserve to be supported.

It's not asking for special or preferential treatment. Having adjustments simply levels the playing field between you and your colleagues, accommodating you to do your job to the best of your ability as best they can.

Disclosure helps to protect you from potential discrimination related to your disability (at any time during your employment). It should also mean that you and your employer hopefully have a more transparent and effective relationship, where you can do your job to the best of your abilities.

There are various points at which you might wish to disclose your ADHD at work, and various examples of adjustments that could help (although these will be unique to every person):

→ **When applying for a job/before an interview:** Some job applications may invite disclosure, and some may be part of a 'Disability Confident' scheme where they guarantee an interview if you meet the minimum requirements of the role. This can be especially useful if you know of adjustments that could be made to support you during the interview process.

> For example, adjustments could include having interview questions provided beforehand, having telephone interviews instead of automatic video interviews with timers, or having extra time to complete assessments.

→ **When starting a job:** You may be asked about disabilities or health conditions upon employment, including anything that could be done to support you.

> Adjustments could include agreeing time to go to medical appointments/therapy, extra training in certain areas, flexible working hours/locations, being given written instructions/feedback, having set deadlines and routines, being given a job coach/mentor with expertise in ADHD, ADHD awareness training for colleagues.

→ **When a problem arises:** ADHD may come up in the workplace due to performance-related or other issues, such as being unable to concentrate. It can also be hard for us to know if ADHD would impact us at work before we're actually doing a job. Your employer should hopefully have an accessible policy explaining how to disclose any health conditions and get support – if not, speak to somebody you trust, or Human Resources.

> Adjustments could include: additional support with challenging areas (such as Excel!), having a job coach to help set a clear structure and time management, ADHD coaching for managers/colleagues, changing the structure of your workload or working patterns, providing a buddy to help with difficult tasks, changing relevant absence policies, and so on.

→ **When you're diagnosed:** If you've been in your job for some time, being diagnosed with ADHD might bring a lot of clarity about struggles you may have faced. However, it might feel intimidating to suddenly speak about this at work, especially if you're in a senior position.

> Adjustments could include discussing the challenges you've faced at work previously and identifying support that could be taken, having a job coach with expertise in ADHD.

→ **Because you want to!** There isn't always the requirement to disclose ADHD for any reason – sometimes we might just want to share more about who we are, empowering others to do the same.

→ **When applying to Access to Work:** For those living in the UK, a Government scheme called Access to Work is available to help people with health conditions at work. It can pay for workplace adjustments such as job coaches, support workers and software, typically involving an online application and independent assessment. If you're employed, your employer would usually be contacted as part of this process.

> Adjustments could include noise-cancelling headphones, software that supports you with time management, electronic notebooks such as Remarkable, job coaching, ADHD awareness training/coaching for colleagues, support workers (including personal assistants), travel expenses, and so on.

The process of disclosing your ADHD at work will be different for everybody depending on their circumstances. Obviously, if you're self-employed, there may not be anyone to disclose to, but if you're employed, your employer should hopefully have a policy setting out the process for discussing health conditions with them. If not, contact us at ADHD Works and we can help your employer to set one up, so that this can help not only you but everybody else who may be in the same position.

If you decide to notify them yourself, you might have a simple discussion about what could support you, or you might be referred to an external 'Occupational Therapist' to advise on how your employer can best accommodate your ADHD at work. This process might feel scary, but remember it's all in place to help you – and external support is available from ADHD Works if you need it.

Remember to tell your employer about Access to Work and apply if relevant – many still don't know about this scheme, and it can identify and pay for adjustments that can be incredibly helpful. We can also help with these processes.

Once you've discussed what adjustments could support you, these should be set up, but I'd recommend writing them down in an email to confirm with the relevant colleagues and asking about when they will be reviewed. Workplace accommodations are an ongoing process and may need changing over time, so please do ensure you know how to ask about this and feel comfortable to do so.

Ultimately, the adjustments that will help you may be very different to ones that might help another person, and they are highly specific to you and your work. Although it can feel like you should have all the answers, often we won't know what can help us until we've tried it out, and so it's important to have an ongoing dialogue about workplace support. It can be helpful to note down all the challenges you experience at work and line these up with how your ADHD impacts you, as in 'A is for ADHD', and discussing this with your employer to see what could help – but this should be a collaborative, supportive discussion.

If you feel unhappy with how you're treated at work in relation to your ADHD, I suggest noting the facts down and speaking to somebody you trust, Acas, a trade union or a legal expert about your options.

How to work through workplace challenges

As we've seen, people with ADHD may struggle staying in employment, especially when things become stressful. We might have difficulty with becoming distracted and procrastinating (see 'P is for Procrastination'), managing our time ('T is for Time Management'), organisation ('O is for Organisation'), boredom ('Q is for Quitting'), maintaining relationships ('L is for Love'), rejection ('R is for Rejection') and impulsivity ('I is for Impulsivity'). The good news is that there are ways around all these challenges – we might just have to do a bit of advance planning!

1. Understand your challenges at work. Write down the things that you have found difficult about work, both in the past and present, such as conflicts with colleagues.

2. Write down ways that you or your employer could actively target these challenges.

   Some examples could include:

   - Wearing noise-cancelling headphones in the office, asking to sit in a quiet area or for flexible working hours/locations so that you can concentrate.

   - Writing out what you want to say in meetings before attending them, which can help in not becoming flustered under pressure in meetings and staying organised.

- Having clear charts of work each week to visibly see the stages of different projects and maintain structure – for example, on a whiteboard or wall planner.

- Asking for help from colleagues in areas that you might struggle, such as data handling.

- Finding out whether your employer has any mental health support policies in place for employees, such as therapy or mindfulness sessions.

- Setting yourself deadlines for work in your calendar to give a sense of urgency, especially for projects that don't have clear timeframes.

- Taking regular breaks and ensuring that you always eat lunch – ideally away from your desk!

- Confirming instructions or requests from colleagues in writing, especially after speaking with them.

Try to set yourself some 'minimum goals', such as staying in a job for a period of time before quitting or identifying one priority 'to do' task to get done each day.

3. Implement your plans and decide whether you want to discuss your ADHD with your employer. A great way of starting a conversation about mental health in the workplace and for stressful periods is making use of the Wellness Action Plans from the organisation Mind.[1]

These are documents that everyone in a team would fill out, writing down how they best cope with stress, what might

---

1   www.mind.org.uk/workplace/mental-health-at-work/taking-care-of-your-staff/employer-resources/wellness-action-plan-download

trigger them to feel worse, and how their colleagues can help. They're an excellent reminder that mental health affects us all – regardless of having ADHD or not. There is also a plan for working from home, which is particularly important as this becomes more common, making us less physically connected to our colleagues, who are an important support system in times of stress.

Self-employment

Many people who have ADHD flourish in self-employment, as they are their own bosses and able to work as they wish. If you struggle with fitting into a 'box', then it can be enormously freeing to be completely in control of your own career; however, it's important to acknowledge areas where you could need help, and to get that help!

There are a few important factors to remember when working for yourself with ADHD:

→ **Consider working with an ADHD coach,** which can be funded by the Government's Access to Work scheme. This can be really helpful for accountability and to ensure you are working as effectively as possible in all areas, including having clear business goals, boundaries and processes for things such as accounting.

→ **Try to avoid spending large amounts of money until you are absolutely sure about your chosen career.** Being self-employed requires a strong sense of financial skill, and being able to save money, as you will generally pay tax at the end of the year! It's a good idea to work with a financial advisor or accountant to ensure that this is taken care of.

→ **Ensure that you have a routine that you stick to,** with clear goals and processes, such as sales and marketing. Being self-employed means that you are your own boss, which requires a strong sense of self-regulation! 'G is for Grounding' can help with this.

→ **Try to find balance.** As in 'H is for Hyper-Focus', it can be tempting to overwork ourselves when we're doing something we're passionate about, which can lead to neglecting our own health and well-being. It's important to keep track of your own working hours and not put too much pressure on yourself!

→ **Create a business plan** and try to think about your long-term goals and priorities.[2]

→ **Don't isolate yourself,** which can be easy to do when we work for ourselves. Try to ensure you're spending as much time as possible with friends and family and doing things you enjoy! If you can, work from a co-working office or coffee shop, so you're around other people.

→ **Track how you spend your time.** Our dopamine-seeking brains might be more driven to the 'fun' work, such as creating social media content, rather than the tasks that are a bit less comfortable, such as following up with sales! Checking in with your priorities regularly is important, as we can easily become distracted without realising!

→ **Delegate work where possible.** Having a virtual assistant is extremely helpful for me to keep on track of processes

---

2 For example, see the Prince's Trust's business plan tips and templates at: www.princes-trust.org.uk/help-for-young-people/tools-resources/ business-tools/business-plans.

and administration, and I have two agencies that help me secure work in different areas to which I pay commission. By identifying your strengths and weaknesses, you can obtain support where relevant – it's investment in yourself!

→ **Remember that it's okay to ask for help.** Seek out mentors or other people in similar areas to you and try to schedule regular phone calls to support each other. Running a business all by yourself is incredibly difficult, and it's important to have someone to hand, even if it is just to offload your stresses onto. You cannot do everything, no matter how hard you try.

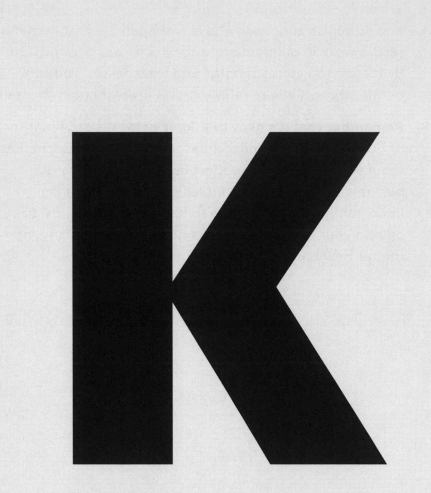

is for Kindness

Did you know?

- It has been proven that people with ADHD suffer from low self-esteem (Mazzone *et al.*, 2013).

- It has been estimated that, by age 12, children who have ADHD receive 20,000 more negative messages from parents, teachers and other adults than their non-ADHD peers (Jellinek, 2010).

- ADHD has been linked with a high risk of self-harm and suicide (Conjero *et al.*, 2019), particularly for adolescent girls (American Psychological Association (APA), 2012).

In my experience, people who have ADHD tend to be extremely kind and compassionate to others. The constant buzzing and overthinking in our brains often revolves around other people and making sure they are all right, and we can prioritise everyone except ourselves.

Whilst this compassion is a wonderful quality to have, it can cause several problems. As seen in 'N is for No', people-pleasing is commonly associated with ADHD and can result in feelings of exhaustion and loneliness. The compassion combined with our quick-thinking minds, enthusiasm for problem-solving and passion for those we love can sometimes also result in offering advice which is not wanted or needed, and can have the opposite effect to helping somebody, which we see more of in 'L is for Love'.

This can be confusing and frustrating for someone who

just wants to help others. It can be very difficult when you are trying your best to be 'nice' in the hope of being liked, accepted and valued by others, and you feel repeatedly rejected for this.

It is almost a distortion of kindness, because we are notoriously terrible at being kind to ourselves. As in an emergency on a flight, you must put your own oxygen mask on first, before helping others. I used to think it was selfish to think of myself over other people, before learning through experience that it's impossible to give from an empty cup, as in 'B is for Burnout'.

ADHD can result in impulsive, self-destructive behaviour. Not thinking things through before acting and chasing adrenaline can result in risky decisions, as in 'V is for Vices'. This is combined with the emotional effects of having ADHD – being hyper-sensitive to rejection, feeling like a failure and unable to commit to anything, beating yourself up for not being able to do simple tasks or for viewing the world differently from everybody else.

So, this chapter is about being kind to yourself and beating the self-destructive thinking. Recognising that you have a right to have your needs met and to be happy is imperative to managing your ADHD symptoms effectively, and also helps the people around you. The people in your life who deserve to be there would much prefer you to be happy looking after yourself rather than unhappy and trying to look after them. When you are your own priority, you will think more about how flippant decisions can affect your long-term happiness. You will prioritise looking after yourself, training yourself to do the boring-but-necessary tasks, organising your life ahead of time, implementing structure and stability. You will choose to beat the negative side-effects of ADHD and learn how to utilise it for your benefit.

Everybody's happiness is their own responsibility. If you are not kind to yourself, you cannot rely on other people to be. It can be extremely difficult to change the way that you think about yourself, because this may be what your life is built upon, such as stories of being unworthy and not good enough. These beliefs might be based on past experiences, but, ultimately, we get to choose what we believe about ourselves and our past. Just because we've had bad experiences doesn't mean we are bad people – we're all doing our best.

You are deserving of love, happiness and acceptance without doing anything at all. You do not have to do anything to be liked by other people, and I guarantee that you have people in your life who love you unconditionally.

A large part of being kind to yourself is re-parenting yourself, as seen in 'O is for Organisation'. Nobody explains to us that when we leave home, we should start parenting ourselves – making sure that we eat healthy, regular meals, live in reasonably clean surroundings, get ourselves to our appointments on time and so on. There are basic human needs that we must meet for ourselves: food, water, air, safety, shelter, human interaction, sleep.

This might sound simple in theory, but in practice it could be quite different. How good are you at cooking or ensuring that you eat three healthy meals a day? How much water do you drink? How often do you take the time to breathe mindfully? How often do you engage in risky behaviour that puts you in danger – such as getting blackout drunk or taking drugs? How about cleaning your house or paying all the bills on time? How's your sleep? How equal are your relationships with others?

The great news is that, by reading this book, you have already started being kind to yourself. Recognising and accepting you may have ADHD is a huge first step in treating yourself with self-compassion.

Having ADHD provides an explanation for the things you might beat yourself up about, such as not being able to do your clothes washing until you have literally nothing left to wear. Accepting that you have been suffering with a neurodevelopmental condition for possibly your entire life changes the foundations on which you have been living. It is not your fault. There is nothing you have done that has 'given' you ADHD.

By accepting this, you can choose to educate yourself and make changes accordingly which will help you to live a happier life. It can be terrifying, when you are only used to darkness, to give yourself the hope of living a life where your happiness is your own priority.

Further on from your basic survival needs, there are those needs that relate to your happiness. Yale University has a class called 'The Science of Well-Being', which identifies scientifically proven key factors for our happiness. These are: meditation, gratitude, savouring, kindness, connection, exercise, sleep and goals.

How are you at taking time for yourself and appreciating the simple things, as in 'Z is for Zen'? How much of your life do you really *live* – fully using your senses, such as eating a piece of cake and fully enjoying how good it tastes? How often are you kind to others with zero expectations in return? How often do you connect with the people around you and show up as yourself in your interactions? How about exercise? How many hours of sleep do you have a night? What long-term goals are you working on?

Please don't be satisfied with just surviving. Choose to live a happy life, to enjoy the time that you have here on this planet. Life is short, and, above all, you are deserving of the kindness that you give to others.

How to be kind to yourself

1. Honestly assess yourself in the below areas:

   - **Sleep:** How many hours you sleep per night, how tired you feel throughout the day.

   - **Eating:** How much you eat in a day, what kind of food you are eating.

   - **Mindfulness:** How often you take the time to be still, such as meditating, journaling or yoga.

   - **Health:** How much alcohol/drugs you consume, how healthy you feel in general.

   - **Exercise:** How often you exercise, the reasons why you exercise.

   - **Home:** How clean is your home, how stable is your home life?

- **Finances:** How often are bills paid on time, do you save money?

- **Social life:** How connected you feel to your friends, family or partner, how lonely you feel.

- **Hobbies:** How much interest you have in your hobbies, how much you enjoy them.

- **Physical appearance:** How you feel about how you look, anything you would like to change.

- **Work:** How much you enjoy your job, what you may prefer to be doing.

- **Happiness:** Overall, how happy you feel with your life at the moment.

2. Notice how you speak to yourself. Go back over the above list and try to spot if you spoke about yourself in a negative way, and note it down, along with any other observations you may have had from assessing your general happiness.

3. Write down the reasons why you may not have been kind to yourself in the past.

4. Write down the *opposite* to your statements above. For example, if you have written, 'I am too lazy to cook myself a healthy meal', write, 'I am *not* lazy'. Find all of the proof for the opposite statement. In our example, this could include 'I get out of bed every morning, have a job, and go to the gym'.

5. Go through the list again and write down how you can improve your happiness in each of the areas – what would be an act of kindness to yourself? Are there any practical

steps you can take from identifying the barriers of being kind to yourself? For example, could you go to sleep earlier, or stay off social media if you find yourself comparing yourself to others? Could you invest more time in what you are interested in, or cut out toxic people who make you feel unhappy?

6. Commit to being kind to yourself and implementing some of the actions above. Make sure steps are achievable, realistic and sustainable at first, but try to set yourself reminders to be kind to yourself, such as reminders on your phone. Some further examples of things you could do to be kind to yourself include:

   - Notice every time you are mean to yourself, either in your head or out loud. Try to catch yourself out and apologise to yourself, changing the statement to be kind to yourself.

   - Ask a friend to call you out every time you say something bad about yourself.

   - Write yourself a love letter, as often as you can.

   - Acknowledge all of the brilliant things about you. Try to give yourself three compliments every day, maybe starting a compliment journal!

   - Celebrate every act of kindness to yourself, however small. Really savour and appreciate when you do something nice for yourself, such as cooking yourself a healthy meal. Take the time to notice how different you feel as a result and appreciate the time and effort you put into yourself.

- Stop people-pleasing! Some people in your life may be unhappy with you suddenly prioritising yourself instead of them and those are the ones who are likely to be exploiting your kindness. No is your new favourite word – see 'N is for No'.

- If you can, allocate some time to yourself each month to do something just for you. You could take yourself out on a date, such as going for a long walk in the park, ordering your favourite meal or getting a massage. Whatever it is, make sure it leaves you feeling happy!

is for Love

Did you know?

- Studies have proven that adult ADHD is associated with difficulties in social relationships and poor negation skills (Moya *et al.*, 2014).

- People with ADHD are more likely to get divorced than those without (Orlov, quoted in Haupt, 2010).

- About 70 per cent of adults reported problems with anger or emotion as part of their ADHD (Nigg, 2020).

ADHD can have a huge impact on our personal relationships, because we think differently to people who don't have ADHD. This isn't necessarily a bad thing, but because we don't typically fit into how 'most' people behave, such as struggling to think about the future or paying attention over a long period of time, misunderstandings can easily arise.

In my experience, the people with ADHD that I know are all incredibly interesting, kind, empathetic and generally wonderful to be around. There's never a boring conversation, they have endless brilliant ideas, they're highly aware of other people's feelings, and they're always interested in many different things.

The challenges associated with ADHD and relationships can impact our self-esteem, but all we can do is try to compromise and show up for the people in our life the best we can. Having ADHD is not our fault, and we're all trying our best. Relationships and intimacy with others can be hard for anyone, but especially when our brains are speeding ahead at a million miles per hour compared to other people's!

Challenges can include:

Hyper-focus

As in 'H is for Hyper-Focus', ADHD-ers have the ability to hyper-focus on activities, interests or people. When I'm extremely passionate about something (like writing this book!) or stressed, it can take over my life for a while, impacting my ability to be fully present with other people. Whilst it might be interesting for them to hear about my current passion, they might also feel like I'm unable to give them my full attention.

It's brilliant to be enthusiastic about life and share interesting topics of conversation, but it is also good for us to be able to regulate this!

We could also become very excited by new people, such as when dating or making new friends, which can feel extremely intense, but wears off over time. This can feel quite sudden if we've got ADHD, leaving us questioning the relationship, and the person we were so enthusiastic about questioning whether we still like them as much. In my experience, this has happened a lot with dating and has been related to diving too quickly into new relationships. Taking things slowly will always build a stronger foundation of trust and connection.

Rejection Sensitive Dysphoria (RSD)

As in 'R is for Rejection', ADHD-ers are very prone to feeling extreme emotional sensitivity and pain triggered by the perception of rejection. This can be very problematic in relationships where we perceive that we are being rejected or disliked, as we may catastrophise and experience 'black-or-white' thinking in such situations. It can result in people-pleasing, as in 'N is for No', where we're putting other people's needs before our own.

For example, when I was a child, I was constantly asking people whether they still liked me! I don't say this out loud any more, but it definitely still makes me feel insecure in my relationships with others, which is probably frustrating for them! It may feel for them as though there's nothing that they can do to convince me they genuinely like me.

This may be due to many friendships in my life ending out of the blue, with me not being able to understand why. The more I've learned about ADHD, the more I've been able to understand these events, but it's resulted in me feeling quite insecure in relationships!

This being said, we tend to be highly empathetic and compassionate in our relationships, but just need skills in having a base level of healthy self-esteem to manage this, as in 'R is for Rejection'.

Time management

ADHD-ers may say yes to invitations automatically, without taking the time to think about whether they are actually able or willing to commit to something. This can result in unintentionally committing to plans we are unable to keep, or lying. White lies can pile on top of white lies when trying to cancel plans without making somebody 'feel bad'.

We can find ourselves cancelling plans or double-booking ourselves, rushing from one appointment to another, without having the time to be present with anybody. We might appear distracted and uninterested in the person we're with, who can feel like a second option.

The difficulties with organisation that accompany ADHD can mean we may struggle to remember appointments or meetings, resulting in unintentionally standing people up or completely forgetting important dates, such as birthdays. I've done this many times, which is always mortifying!

Communication

ADHD can also appear as rudeness, with a tendency to speak before we think, and challenges with listening, given the impairments on our inhibition, memory and self-awareness, as in 'E is for Executive Functioning'. We might be prone to saying things that we don't mean or interrupting others, and find it hard to focus on conversations – I am forever 'zoning out'!

This can also lead to forgetting appointments with others and asking questions we've already been told the answers to, making the other person feel that we're not listening to them.

In my experience, ADHD-ers don't deal particularly well with silence, and may blurt things out to fill any gaps in conversation, in the hope of making the other person feel comfortable. This can sometimes emerge as oversharing, which can result in unequal relationships.

We may also struggle with small talk. I often find myself asking quite random questions in conversations such as

'What would you do if you won the lottery?', which I've been told can feel like a therapy session – but is definitely never boring!

Arguments

Arguments are a normal part of any relationship, but the strong emotional reactions associated with ADHD can result in explosive arguments. ADHD-ers may really struggle with understanding and regulating their own emotions and communicating calmly.

An understanding of how ADHD can manifest is really important here for both ADHD-ers and the people in our lives, because it allows us to compromise and have empathy for each other. People don't typically have negative intentions towards us, but being able to calmly explain how we feel and what we need can sometimes be very challenging for everyone, especially people with ADHD! Arguments may also arise out of small misunderstandings or repeated mistakes, such as being late, which may be due to our ADHD. Personally, I've had many arguments about me being messy, even when I'd made a huge effort to clean up – I simply didn't see mess like the other person did!

It can also be good for us to have an outlet to process our emotions, such as attending therapy sessions, journaling or having a regular form of exercise. I'm often surprised by my own emotions which can build up and strike without warning if I don't do these things, which can feel like reverting to being a toddler having a tantrum! Arguments can be dangerous for an ADHD-er due to our impaired inhibition, which can see us making decisions we'd later regret, such as quitting a job or cutting someone out of our life. Although we might calm down later, the other person might not! I recommend treating yourself like a small child in this instance and trying to ensure you have space to calm down before making any big decisions – for example, by going for a walk when you feel overwhelmed.

Loneliness

Having ADHD can be incredibly lonely. It is very difficult for other people to understand you if they do not have full awareness or acceptance of ADHD, especially if you aren't diagnosed. It can be hard for someone to believe that you physically cannot listen to them for an extended period, no matter how hard you try. Or that you literally cannot bring yourself to look at your bank account, clean your bedroom or keep track of your appointments. For a person without ADHD, these are simply matters of 'motivation'. ADHD-ers might often find themselves being referred to as lazy by frustrated people in their life, who don't understand that this is a serious medical condition.

This can lead to us feeling invalidated by the people in our life, who may not be able to understand what we're going through. It might be very challenging for those of us diagnosed as adults to fully communicate this experience to other people, especially those who have known us for our entire lives. Personally, I've often felt like I've had to 'prove' it to other people, especially those who don't 'believe' in ADHD.

Eventually, I learned that this just isn't possible in some situations, as I'd always feel insecure about such a vital part of who I am – so I try to only have people in my life who validate my experiences, as much as possible!

Unsurprisingly, social anxiety is often seen in ADHD-ers, especially given how much stigma there is in relation to ADHD. It can feel much easier to exclude yourself from the world than to have the pressures of socialising in polite society. I've felt a tremendous amount of anxiety around my family and friends as a result of my ADHD. I couldn't bear to explain to people what I had 'been up to' since the last time they saw me – it could involve anything from moving country to starting a new business and giving it all up!

It is incredibly hard to believe in yourself if you think that nobody else does either. Social connections are an extremely important aspect of being happy. You deserve to have good relationships with your friends and family, and to receive the love back that you provide to them.

Navigating ADHD in relationships

Based on my personal experiences, the below advice may be helpful:

Identifying our own needs

As we have impairments in self-awareness, it can be very challenging to understand what we need or want in certain situations, especially if something happens very quickly.

I've found it very helpful to ensure I have the space to reflect on these things every day, such as by doing yoga and journaling. Being clear on what we need enables us to set boundaries with people on how we want to be treated in relationships, and to ensure we're taking responsibility for our own well-being.

Communicating clearly

I can find it very hard to communicate with others, especially if I'm feeling emotional, as this impairs my executive functioning skills and ability to think clearly, let alone interact with someone else. I've heard of neurotypical people having 'holding boxes' in their brains where they think of what they say before they say it, but I definitely don't have that! I'm often finding out what I think at the same time as other people, which isn't always very helpful for our relationship.

For this, it's been very helpful for me to have reference points, such as writing out agendas for important conversations. As I communicate best by writing, it can also be useful for me to interact with others in this way in certain situations.

Another tool for communicating with other people is by saying, 'When you do/say X, I feel Y. I would prefer it if you did Z'. This helps us to explain how we feel without assuming any responsibility on the other person. We're explaining how their behaviour makes us feel and asking clearly for what we'd prefer to happen.

Ultimately, slowing down the time we take to speak our thoughts out loud can enable us to be mindful about how we interact with other people, such as by counting to a certain number before speaking.

Understanding our ADHD

It was only when I began to understand my own brain

that I could explain it to other people, which is part of the reason I wrote this book! It's up to you to decide whether you feel comfortable sharing this with others, but I do suggest taking responsibility for the parts of it that can impact other people.

It's not our fault we have ADHD, but it is our responsibility to manage it once we know about it. It doesn't give us an 'excuse' to treat other people without respect, but it empowers us to understand how we might naturally act and decide how we want to be. Ironically, learning about this probably gives us a much deeper level of self-awareness than a neurotypical person!

Trusting people slowly

An important lesson for ADHD-ers is that trust is earned, not automatically granted, and we should only share personal information with people that we trust and who we feel have earned the right to hear it.

This is particularly relevant to our impairment in inhibition and working memory, as in 'E is for Executive Functioning', which can make us very trusting of other people. We might not learn from our experiences as other people do due to forgetting them!

The secret to this is getting to know somebody slowly and trying to identify clear examples over time that prove you can trust this person. This is particularly important in our world where it's normalised to meet strangers from the internet, such as on dating apps! Try to slow down the 'getting to know you' phase as much as you can – I promise it'll be better in the long term!

Learning to listen

From becoming an ADHD coach, I learned the immense value of listening to someone and asking questions, especially instead of offering solutions. This is an important part of being in a reciprocal relationship, where we're able to spend time with people we care about and validate each other's experiences.

To overcome challenges with concentration during conversations, it can be helpful to identify ways you concentrate better. For example, I try to always be doodling or writing notes during meetings and fidgeting with jewellery when talking to other people. It can also be helpful to remind yourself to keep looking into people's eyes when talking to them, as this can better hold our focus.

Asking for help

If people don't know we're struggling, they can't help! Many ADHD-ers can struggle with asking for help, given our avoidance of potential sources of rejection and low self-esteem. However, this is a crucial part of having healthy relationships – having someone be there for you as you would be for them.

I've found this to be especially important when I burn out, for example, and look like I'm doing really well from the outside. Friends can become frustrated with me cancelling plans, but it's only when I explain that I'm not in a very good place that they can truly understand and offer support.

Not trying to do it all

Human beings aren't designed to have thousands of connections, as we do today on social media. This can leave us feeling overwhelmed and exhausted in trying to keep up with lots of different people, let alone remembering our different conversations with them all!

I've learned that having a few strong relationships (and prioritising these in real life!) is much more sustainable for me than trying to be friends with everyone. This also enabled me to properly ensure I have people in my life who I genuinely enjoy spending time with and care deeply for, rather than trying to please everyone and having lots of surface-level relationships!

Setting boundaries

As in 'N is for No', boundaries are the invisible lines between us and other people – they are us teaching others how we want to be treated. Being able to set clear boundaries in our relationships, such as understanding what we do and do not expect from others, enables us to understand whether someone is respecting us.

This can be thought of as a house, where we choose who enters our space and on what terms, such as metaphorically asking people to take their shoes off. The door isn't shut forever, but we decide when to open and close it. I've found this very helpful to help me regain a sense of control over some unhealthy relationships, in setting expectations that I feel comfortable with, such as seeing some people in certain settings, rather than being constantly available to them.

Activities you can do to improve your relationships include:

→ **Create a 'communication plan' for certain people in your life that you trust.** This could explain how your

ADHD impacts you, what to do if they're worried about you, and how they can best help you, especially during an argument. This sort of advance planning can help us manage stressful situations, where we all react in different ways.

→ **Take responsibility for the parts of your ADHD that are causing issues with other people,** such as being late, by identifying these and thinking of a solution to implement – just do one at a time! For example, you could ask people to tell you a time to meet that's half an hour earlier than when they actually want to meet, or build this time in yourself, if lateness is a problem.

→ **Remember that relationships are two-way, and we have to both put effort in.** Having ADHD isn't a 'problem', but can simply result in different ways of thinking, so it's good to be able to find a compromise. However, try not to allow others to make you feel as though there's anything wrong with you for having ADHD. Just by reading this book, you're probably more self-aware than many other people. These symptoms show up in all of us in one way or another, just to different degrees!

→ **Write a letter or have a conversation with the people in your life that you want to improve your relationships with,** acknowledging the impact that the relationship has in your life and thanking the person for being there. Be careful not to over-apologise for things you haven't done – we can often place a lot of unnecessary blame on ourselves.

→ **Read 'N is for No' to stop people-pleasing.** Only say what you mean and mean what you say. Don't commit to things mindlessly or because you feel that you should.

→ **Use your calendar for your personal life,** such as setting reminders for people's birthdays and arrangements to meet up.

→ **Make an effort to really listen to people when they talk, and maintain eye contact.** A good way of doing this is repeating each word they say in your head, instead of trying to think of what to say in response.

→ **Ensure that you have a period of free time for yourself each week,** even just half an hour. Make sure that your own battery is charged before giving energy to others, as in 'K is for Kindness'.

→ **Seek out the support of a therapist and/or ADHD coach** to help you find balance and healthy routines in your relationships with other people. Therapy is very important for us to have a space to process our emotions.

→ **If you're having issues in specific relationships, try seeing a therapist together.** I found couple's therapy to be incredibly helpful for me to see that not everything was my fault!

→ **If people in your life are not supportive about your ADHD, I'd recommend thinking about your options.** For example, I've dated people who didn't agree with me taking ADHD medication, which made me question myself and my doctor's advice! This may not be realistic for all relationships, but please remember to prioritise yourself and your health first – if someone doesn't make you feel safe in talking about your ADHD with them, reconsider your boundaries with this person.

→ **If this applies to a work context, have a look at 'J is for Jobs'.** You should never be discriminated against because of your ADHD, especially at work.

→ **Think about all of your brilliant qualities and why the people in your life are lucky to have you.** Having ADHD can feel overwhelming, but, ultimately, it makes us interesting, supportive, passionate and caring people. Remember that your worth comes from inside, not outside, and you are loved by the people in your life, who are lucky to have you! Seek out support groups and other people who have ADHD, as in 'U is for Unite'. This can be helpful for us to feel validated and connect with others who share our experiences. If you're particularly hyper-focused on something, you could also find a community for this.

is for Medication

Did you know?

- In the UK, healthcare providers should ensure that people with ADHD have a 'comprehensive, holistic shared treatment plan that addresses psychological, behavioural and occupational or educational needs' (National Institute for Health and Care Excellence, 2019). This demonstrates that medication by itself is not enough to treat ADHD – there should also be lifestyle adaptions where necessary.

- ADHD stimulant medication has been proven to be very effective, with a responsiveness rate of 70–80 per cent (Spencer *et al.*, 2005). Stimulant medication helps the neurotransmitters in the ADHD brain that are not working so well to function better.

- A range of non-pharmacological solutions have been linked with positive effects on ADHD symptoms, including therapy, fish oil, exercise and getting enough sleep. Though the condition may change over time, it's with us for life, as ADHD cannot be outgrown.

Medication can be very tricky to navigate for ADHD-ers who struggle with self-awareness, executive functioning and bureaucracy. When I was diagnosed and prescribed medication by a private psychiatrist I didn't even have a GP in the UK, due to moving country so often! From battling with the stigma surrounding ADHD medication to the administrative challenges in accessing it each month, to observing how it impacts your body and understanding your options, it can be an incredibly frustrating minefield.

As I am not a medical professional, this chapter doesn't go into the formal details of ADHD medication. Instead, it shares my experiences and the support I wish I'd had when I started taking it.

Taking medication is a deeply personal choice, which I recommend discussing with your doctor. Although you are ultimately the only person that you can trust when it comes to understanding your own body, the medication can be life-changing for managing ADHD symptoms. Please do try the medication that your doctor suggests, avoid self-medicating, and be patient – it can take a while to find the right type for you, but trust in the process.

Just as you'd take medication for a physical health condition such as diabetes or cancer, you deserve to receive this same support for a neurodevelopmental condition if its symptoms are impairing your life. Help is available, and it's what *you* decide that matters – nobody else.

My experience

When I was first diagnosed, I felt very conflicted and scared about taking ADHD medication. I thought it would make me weak, was terrified of becoming dependent on it, and felt a lot of shame around having to take medication just to be 'normal'.

However, when I tried it out, it felt like putting on glasses after not being able to see for my entire life. I could literally see dust all over my flat, and the 500 thoughts that usually were competing for my attention at any one time disappeared. I could actually listen to someone and focus on what they were saying, felt stronger in my body and could easily do the things I usually avoided, such as exercising.

I was amazed to experience that 'normal' for other people meant not having a constant radio blasting 15 different channels 24 hours per day through their brains.

However, it has definitely not been easy, especially because I didn't feel like I had anyone to speak to about the process properly. I didn't know anyone else with ADHD. I spoke to lots of different people about it, some of whom made me feel quite embarrassed.

As I was prescribed medication privately, it cost me hundreds of pounds to speak to the psychiatrist and access the prescription each month, which made me feel like I couldn't reach out to them properly for advice. As a result of my own confusion, I started only taking it on certain days instead of as prescribed, which made me very unwell.

Things became much better once I signed up to a local GP and worked collaboratively with them on my treatment. It's really important to have regular professional medical oversight of any new medication by a doctor that you can reach out to when needed.

Now, having taken the right dose of medication consistently for over three years, I can say with absolute certainty that it has changed my life for the better. When I wasn't taking it, I was constantly moving job and country, arguing with people in my life and making impulsive decisions I later regretted. I felt highly anxious all the time.

In comparison, over the last few years, I've managed to focus enough to find stability. I've not only been able to finish writing books like this one, but I've also managed to find peace, live with much less anxiety, think through decisions properly, have strong relationships and live a much happier life. This definitely isn't just due to medication, but all of the things I've done to treat my ADHD along the way, like coaching and lifestyle changes. It's been like a jigsaw puzzle, and the right medication has definitely been a part of that.

These days, I treat my medication like a daily vitamin, and don't think about it too much in comparison to when I was first diagnosed.

I now trust my own experiences first and foremost. The proof of this for me is in the evidence of how different my life is now compared to before I started taking this medication and building my jigsaw.

Stigma and ADHD medication

There is a huge amount of stigma relating to taking medication for our mental health, and especially for conditions such as ADHD. It can feel confusing to be offered medication simply because you think differently to other people, but, ultimately, if your ADHD is having a significantly negative impact on your life, there is no shame in taking medication to change that.

I worked through the stigma I experienced by prioritising my own health above the opinions of others, which I still have to do every so often. It can feel as though I am 'cheating' somehow by taking medication, and I have to remind myself that taking it just means that my brain is able to operate like everybody else's.

For example, I know that I managed to get As in my exams before being medicated, but now, when I do a course, I can actually process and retain the information being taught.

The way to deal with medication-related anxiety is to be compassionate and kind to yourself, as in 'K is for Kindness'. If you had a broken arm, you would use a sling. You would do whatever you could to get better as quickly as possible. You wouldn't expect to be able to live the rest of your life with one arm instead, just because you theoretically could. If someone advised you not to use the sling and to just try harder to mend the bones through willpower, you probably wouldn't react too well!

If your partner had heart disease, you'd be making sure they took their prescribed medication every single day. Yet, with mental health, it is often another story – because it is invisible, we don't treat it in the same way. Taking medication does not make you weak – it literally makes you stronger. Having ADHD is nothing to be ashamed about, as in 'W is for Weaknesses'.

The medication activates the neurotransmitters in your brain responsible for self-regulation, which is why people who have ADHD have been known to self-medicate with alcohol, drugs, smoking and caffeine. Before I took my medication, I used to smoke, drink ten coffees per day, and binge-drink alcohol to an extremely unhealthy degree, but now I don't need these things at all. In fact, even one coffee now has a huge effect on me when I've taken my medication.

Personally, I'd much prefer to take the medication prescribed to me by a doctor that enables me to make sensible decisions, such as not to take illegal drugs, rather than unconsciously self-medicating on addictive, dangerous and illegal substances to manage my ADHD symptoms.

Taking medication prescribed by your doctor has zero correlation to your self-worth. At the same time, *not* taking medication has zero correlation to your self-worth – it is ultimately up to you.

As ADHD medication has become even more controversial in recent years, especially in the media, I'd strongly recommend trying to listen to your *own* opinion about it. Instead of searching for answers by talking to everybody you know like I did, I suggest carefully choosing a few people you trust and sharing your experiences with them.

Having ADHD can impact our own self-awareness, as in 'Y is for Your Body', so I'd also recommend keeping a medication diary whilst trying any new types. You could record any side-effects, how you feel and any changes in certain symptoms, such as concentration levels. By keeping this by your bed, you can remind yourself to fill it in every evening before going to sleep.

Managing your ADHD medication

In the UK, any medication for ADHD must be originally prescribed by a specialist psychiatrist, not a GP. There may be an initial 'titration' period, where you're closely monitored to see how different types or doses of medication work for you. ADHD manifests differently in everybody and there is no one 'cure all' tablet – different medication will work for different people, and you might need to try a few to find the one that is right for you.

Once a point has been reached where your psychiatrist is happy, they can refer you back to your GP, as in 'D is for Diagnosis', for 'shared care', which means they can continue prescribing you the medication you've already been taking.

This does mean that you'll have to return to the psychiatrist for changes outside of what has been prescribed, which is when my GP told me it would take seven years through their NHS waiting list!

There are different kinds of ADHD medication, but it tends to be highly regulated as a 'controlled drug'. This means that, in the UK, doctors will not prescribe more than one month's worth at a time.

This could be helpful as a metaphorical anchor, as in 'G is for Grounding' (it's much harder for me to spontaneously move country now!), but difficult if you have trouble with organisation, routines and attending appointments – which many people with ADHD do!

It can also be hard for us to even remember to take the medication each day, especially if we've got more than one tablet to take, or certain times of day to remember.

It's also important that your doctor properly monitors your use of the medication, taking your weight and blood pressure regularly, because the side-effects can be dangerous.

Now I see my doctor every three months for a physical check-up and call every month for a repeat prescription, which is sent directly to the pharmacy. It has taken a lot of refinement to get to this point, and was overwhelming at first, but it's just a matter of explaining your situation and asking for help when needed.

I recommend discussing this with your doctor, or possibly an ADHD coach, to help you build up a monthly streamlined routine to manage your ADHD medication. For example, it could include:

→ **Asking your doctor about what you should expect** and if there's anything to be aware of, such as certain side-effects or times to contact them.

→ **Setting reminders on your calendar for you to check in with your doctor each month to renew your prescription.** You could highlight months where you might need to have an in-person review of your medication.

→ **Setting reminders on your calendar to go to the pharmacy on the same day each month to pick up your prescription.** You could also ask your pharmacist to call you as a reminder. Sometimes they might need to order the medication in once you have the prescription, so advance warning is always helpful, as is a good relationship with your pharmacist!

→ **Setting alarms on your phone for taking medication,** especially if it's at certain times of the day. I strongly recommend taking your medication at the same time every day.

→ **Asking a family member, friend, or coach to check in with you** a week in advance of your medication running out, to ensure you've ordered your prescription.

→ **Using a medication box with days of the week written on it,** to ensure you've taken your medication each day. You could set a weekly reminder to fill this back up again!

→ **Speaking to your doctors about the best way you can organise your prescription** each month and alerting them to any holidays in advance.

→ **Keeping your medication in a place where you can easily access it,** such as by your toothbrush.

→ **Keeping a medication log** and discussing this with your doctor.

→ **Ensuring you read and follow the instructions of any new medication properly,** possibly asking a family member or friend to read it too. I didn't do this and really regretted it later on when I couldn't sleep after drinking coffee!

→ **Learning about the potential side-effects of medication and taking relevant actions,** such as ensuring you eat three meals per day if it impacts your appetite.

→ **Never giving anyone else your medication to take** – this can be extremely dangerous and even illegal.

→ **Having an emergency tablet in a designated wallet on you at all times,** or where you can easily access it, such as at work or a partner's house.

→ **Making relevant lifestyle changes.** These might include starting coaching or not drinking alcohol, for example. Medication should be one part of a much broader holistic approach, and this is often the most important part of overcoming ADHD challenges.

It can be tempting to try and constantly assess whether medication is 'working', but I strongly advise trying not to ruminate on this. It's natural to feel anxious about taking any medication, especially if you've had to wait a long time to access it, it's really expensive and is a 'controlled' drug, as is often the case with ADHD medication! However, the effects are *supposed* to make you feel 'normal'. There can be a lot of stigma around medication, but ultimately I recommend doing what feels right for you. Approach it like drinking coffee – don't overthink it! Therapy or coaching can help with this.

It is extremely important that you speak to your doctor as soon as possible if you feel depressed or concerned, or do not experience the expected effects. If something doesn't feel right, tell someone you trust as soon as possible and get professional help. Trust yourself, check in with your body regularly, and remember that it can take some time to figure out the right dose and type of medication for you.

ADHD medication is unlikely to be an overnight 'fix', and it won't 'cure' your symptoms, but it should help you manage certain symptoms. It's important to take a holistic approach, and there are other things that can help support you with your ADHD that aren't medication.

ADHD coaching

I explain ADHD coaching and medication with an analogy of wanting to repair a jumper for your entire life, but never having been able to. One day, you're given glasses and can see the holes you were previously unable to see, but you still don't know how to sew. This is where a coach comes in, to support you in learning how to do that.

They're not supposed to be there forever, but just long enough for you to learn these skills, holding you accountable and ensuring they're fully implemented in your brain.

For example, when I first took my medication, I could suddenly see mess in my flat properly for what felt like the first time ever. However, I still didn't know how to clean it up properly. I didn't know how to hoover, at what point to clean each week, what types of cleaning products I needed, or what I needed to do. I could just suddenly see the mess that everybody else kept referring to!

ADHD coaches help you to use these new powers, because pills don't give skills. There's not necessarily much use in suddenly being able to better concentrate if we're choosing to focus on things like social media instead of work!

An ADHD coach can help with implementing skills of self-regulation to manage our brains and should have specialised knowledge of what can help ADHD-ers. For example, I trained with ADD Coaching Academy, which has a very intensive coaching course spanning several hours per week and assessments over a number of months.

In the UK, the Government can fund 100 per cent of an ADHD coach if you're in employment through Access to Work, as in 'J is for Jobs'. I personally found ADHD coaching to be the most helpful thing I've ever done for my own understanding of ADHD and learning to thrive *because* of it, not in spite of it. So much so that I became an ADHD coach myself!

I've seen my clients have the same experiences from having an independent person with knowledge of ADHD support them in learning and implementing strategies to transform their lives. I've coached people on everything from cleaning out their houses to organising their workloads and managing Rejection Sensitive Dysphoria to coordinating all of their brilliant ideas. Coaching is very forward-focused and practical, and isn't supposed to be forever – it's meant to teach you how to fish for yourself, instead of feeding you for a day.

It's important to find the right coach for you, and most offer free introductory sessions to see if you get on. It's important to note that anybody can call themselves a coach and it's a largely unregulated industry. Please ensure you check with any coach about their experience and, in particular, their knowledge of ADHD, before starting.

Ultimately, the most important thing is that you trust your coach and are willing to put the work in around the sessions to make the changes you want to see.

Therapy

In contrast to the practical nature of coaching, therapy can help with processing emotional issues such as depression, anxiety and self-limiting beliefs. It's really important to have on an ongoing basis to give yourself the space to process your emotions in a contained way.

It's important to find the right therapist for you, especially because we might be discussing very sensitive and deeply personal information with them.

Therapy can be expensive and difficult to stick to if we don't feel that it is immediately helpful. The main benefit of therapy is having somebody to simply listen to us, and the benefits are often seen over a longer period, which can be a challenge for those of us who are seeking instant gratification or advice! Looking backwards and inspecting our thoughts can also lead us to ruminate and spark up lots of emotions, so please do ensure your therapist is able to help you manage this if it happens.

If you can find a therapist with understanding of ADHD and who is pro-active, this will be ideal. I've found 'alternative' therapies to be incredibly helpful, which keeps me interested with the novelty aspect, such as music and art therapy with a therapist called Talia Girton.[1] Playing for no other reason than having fun in therapy and keeping our brains stimulated is like ADHD gold!

Other kinds of therapy, such as Cognitive Behavioural Therapy, can be very useful, as this provides skills to change how you think and behave. However, it may require you to do homework around the sessions, so it's important to flag your ADHD with the therapist and ask for extra support or accountability where needed (speaking from experience!).

Your GP may be able to refer you for therapy on the NHS, so definitely ask them if they don't do this automatically. As with coaching, it's important to find a therapist who is properly qualified, so please do explore your options and ask lots of questions before getting started.

Diet

The food that we put into our bodies can have an enormous effect on our minds. For minds that are searching for stimulation, sugar, caffeine and alcohol can easily hit the

---

1   www.taliagirton.com

sweet spot. The problem with this is that these energy highs are short-lived, addictive and terrible for our bodies – there's a strong link between obesity and ADHD (Olivardia, 2018). I used to live on chocolate bars and coffee, which caused me to be exhausted and weak. Sugary drinks can seem like an instant hit of energy and focus, but the effect quickly wears off to leave us depleted and tired.

For ADHD-ers, cooking can seem a bit long-winded and boring. I used to be terrible at following recipes and would just throw in a rough guess of the measurements required. This usually ended up with slightly weird-tasting food and a messy kitchen that I would be unable to muster up the energy to clean. Eating take-out and food grabbed on the go was much easier.

However, like chocolate, this 'fast food' gives us short energy spikes, followed by exhaustion. ADHD-ers can often suffer with sleep problems, as in 'S is for Sleep', and having a diet of sugar and caffeine only makes these problems worse. It's also expensive to buy food out or order it in every day, which can quickly add up, as seen in 'F is for Finances'.

Learning to cook is one of the best things you can do for yourself. Incorporating cooking and proper time to eat meals into your routine, as in 'G is for Grounding', will change your life and allow you to be in control of your energy instead of being at the mercy of sugar and caffeine.

It's a good idea to try to eliminate as much sugar, coffee, alcohol and fast food as you can from your diet. By planning meals and thinking about where you might usually snack on unhealthy food, you can figure out how to overcome your blocks. For example, if you don't have the time to make breakfast in the morning, make it the night before!

If you struggle with buying ingredients, you could invest in a food delivery service, such as Oddbox or Gousto, or plan this out in advance each week. You can also use a slow cooker to cook one big meal each weekend that you can eat the entire week without thinking about it, which removes the stress of planning out different meals. Dedicating just a little time each weekend to your diet for the week ahead will have a significant impact on your life and health.

Exercise

Studies have shown that regular physical activity can decrease the severity of ADHD symptoms and improve cognitive functioning (Hillman *et al.*, 2019). Exercise can do the same thing for the brain as ADHD medication does, at least for a short period of time. It also produces endorphins, making us feel happy, and allows us to burn off our excess energy – which ADHD-ers have a lot of! It calms us down, clears our minds, and makes us 'be' in our bodies, helping us to focus on one thing.

However, if you're anything like me, you might struggle to motivate yourself to exercise! I overcame this by figuring out how to make it as easy and enjoyable as possible, whether that's sleeping in my gym clothes or trying out trapeze and silent disco classes. Having exercise buddies or joining a team can also be helpful for accountability.

I'd strongly recommend incorporating exercise into your daily routine any way that you can, even if it's just walking instead of getting public transport or having a stretch before bed. It'll clear your mind and burn off any excess energy you might have, allowing you to focus better throughout the day and sleep well at night.

Mindfulness

Mindfulness is a great way to train your brain and some forms, such as 'meditative mindfulness' have also been proven to have a positive effect on ADHD symptoms (Mitchell *et al.,* 2017). This refers to being in the present moment and consciously choosing your thoughts instead of allowing them to infiltrate your mind at all times. Slowing down and being present can be very difficult for an ADHD-er, but there are ways of hacking mindfulness to work for you, as in 'Z is for Zen'.

Being kind to yourself, as in 'K is for Kindness', is another very important factor in improving your ADHD. Self-compassion allows us to reason with our own minds to change our negative behaviours, because this will result in the best scenario for us. When we fundamentally care about ourselves, we will want to make sure that we eat proper food or live in a clean environment or stay in a stable job. When we recognise that we deserve to be happy, we can turn our attention to figuring out the best way of finding and keeping that happiness.

is for No

Did you know?

- Many people with ADHD suffer from emotional dysregulation, hyper-sensitivity to rejection and low self-esteem. ADHD-ers may struggle with saying no or thinking things through properly before saying yes, in order to please others. As in 'Y is for Your Body', sensory issues can accompany ADHD which can contribute to us not being able to understand our own needs on even the most basic levels – which then can't be communicated to others!

- ADHD has been linked to problems in processing communication, resulting in misunderstandings with others. For example, zoning out during a conversation, or having memory problems causing ADHD-ers to forget what they have previously said. This can result in shame and 'white lies' in an attempt to fix the situation, often manifesting as people-pleasing (Bernstein, 2010).

- The Rejection Sensitive Dysphoria that is said to accompany ADHD can result in people with ADHD becoming people-pleasers. Dr William Dodson said people with RSD 'quickly scan every person they meet and have a remarkable ability to figure out exactly what that person would admire or praise... they are so intent on avoiding the possibility of displeasure from others and keeping everyone happy that they often lose track of their own desires' (Dodson, 2016).

Having a quick mind that tends to act before thinking things through properly means that ADHD-ers can be prone to committing to things that we might not actually want to do and saying things that we don't mean. Combined with other ADHD symptoms such as having a short attention span and being hyper-sensitive to possible rejection, this can mean that we feel desperate for the acceptance of other people, and will do anything to get it.

This results in people-pleasing – putting other people before yourself, acting out of 'feeling bad' or wanting to be 'nice'. It can feel like subconsciously choosing to exploit yourself for others in the hope that they will like you. It can mean that we struggle with saying no or setting boundaries in relationships, and we over-exert ourselves, impacting all areas of our lives.

The irony in this is that people rarely react the way that you want them to, despite your best efforts. Nobody can control how another person feels. Some people are not going to like you and that is the end of it – there isn't any amount of flowers, notes or kindness that you can give them to change their minds. Ironically, you can often actually end up pleasing nobody at all, because you are so exhausted from spreading yourself so thinly that you actually can't fully commit to anything or anyone, as in 'B is for Burnout'.

Another way that people-pleasing can affect relationships is by lying. We might try to get out of tricky situations with a white lie or an excuse, because we feel too 'bad' saying the truth – such as we simply don't want to see someone. Due to our impulsivity, this could happen before we've even consciously realised, which can be incredibly frustrating.

These lies can be hard to keep track of and are easily found out, like a child with chocolate all over their face saying they haven't eaten any! This can also manifest as overpromising or setting impossible expectations on ourselves that we cannot meet, perpetuating feelings of insecurity and guilt.

Struggling with saying no has led me to end up feeling resentful, as though all my relationships were based on me doing things for other people, never having any time for myself to do things like cook or exercise, becoming physically unwell as a result, and feeling generally overwhelmed.

People-pleasing has become embedded into our society, which values 'busyness' over having time to relax, and being a 'good' person, employee, friend, family member and so on – essentially, being able to do it all. These unrealistic expectations are exacerbated by social media, where we are reachable 24 hours, seven days a week. You are simply a human being at the end of the day, and only have a limited capacity in how much you can do – and your first priority needs to be you. By valuing yourself, you will be guided as to what and who else you should be valuing in your life, instead of automatically accepting everything.

Boundaries

To stop people-pleasing, it's necessary for us to set, communicate and uphold boundaries. Boundaries are the invisible lines we draw between us and other people, enabling us to have healthy relationships.

Boundaries can be explicitly stated, such as the number of hours you're contracted to work in a week, or implicit, such as offering a person your hand to shake, instead of holding out your arms for a hug.

Boundaries can be:

→ **Porous:** Which tend to be poorly expressed, such as saying yes to things we don't want to do. I've struggled with this immensely to the point of often working for free.

→ **Rigid:** Which tend to be inflexible in all situations and result in people being held at a distance, such as never attending any social events. For example, I've cut friends out of my life quite harshly after feeling rejected by them, out of anxiety.

→ **Healthy:** Which tend to be made with an awareness of our own capabilities and capacities, with clear communication, and consciously based from the present moment. For example, this could look like sharing with people that you trust, when it feels appropriate to do so.

They could also be:

→ **Material:** Such as expecting people to ask before borrowing our belongings.

→ **Physical:** Involving our physical space, such as a person asking our permission before they touch us.

→ **Emotional:** Which can relate to not taking on other people's emotions and taking responsibility for how we feel, without expecting others to make us feel better.

→ **Intellectual:** Such as having our own opinions, showing up on time and communicating when we're running late.

When we set boundaries, we must also communicate them

and act to uphold them. I've found with my ADHD that I have to work extra hard at even identifying them in the first place, given the impairment to my self-awareness in being able to identify my needs, as in 'E is for Executive Functioning'.

Prioritising yourself

As ADHD-ers can struggle with time management, impulsivity and distraction, we can forget to prioritise ourselves, especially when somebody is making a request of us.

Essentially, this requires us to have self-awareness and an ability to identify how we want to live our own lives, instead of reacting to external events. Instead of externalising our focus in life on other people, we can focus it on ourselves.

This can be achieved by:

1. Writing out a list of your non-negotiable *needs* in the following areas:

    - **Sleep:** How many hours do you need a night to feel rested? Is this ever interrupted by people-pleasing – such as accepting invitations to go out every night, even if you don't want to?

    - **Eating:** How do you plan to cook and eat your meals each day? What do you need to do each week to prioritise your meals, such as dedicating time for this on the weekends?

    - **Mindfulness:** How often do you relax and have uninterrupted time to do 'nothing'?

    - **Health:** What do you need to do to feel healthy each

day? When do you exercise? Do you need to take medication each day, and prioritise any medical appointments?

- **Home:** What do you need from your living environment? Are you a clean or messy person? How much time do you need to spend alone vs socialising with people you live with?

- **Finances:** How much money do you need to survive? What do you need to prioritise in terms of spending? How much do you spend on yourself? What are your minimum rates for work? Do you charge for overtime?

- **Social life:** How much interaction with friends and family do you need to feel connected? How much time do you want to dedicate to this each week?

- **Dating:** What do you need in a relationship to feel secure and happy? How do you want to be treated by somebody you're dating?

- **Hobbies:** What hobbies do you need to make you happy? How often are you consciously enjoying your life?

- **Physical boundaries:** What do you feel comfortable with in terms of other people being close to you?

- **Work:** What do you need from your job? Are you doing anyone else's job, or taking on too much at work? What are your working hours? Can colleagues contact you outside of those times?

2. Assessing the areas listed above and identifying how often your needs get met. Do you find yourself prioritising other people in certain areas? Can you imagine these needs

filling up your energy like a rechargeable battery and frame them as necessary for you to be able to properly give to other people?

3. Making a list of core needs you've identified as present form statements. For example:

    *   I have eight hours of sleep each night.

    *   My working hours are 9am–5pm, and I do not check my emails outside of these hours.

    *   I socialise on these days of the week.

    *   I dedicate time on Sundays to cooking my food for the week ahead.

    *   I keep this night of the week free.

4. Keeping this list somewhere you can see it and read it out loud to yourself in the mirror, noticing how it feels. Can you imagine you're reading it about somebody else? How does this change things?

5. Trying to set aside some time to do this regularly, changing your list where necessary or where you might need some extra reminders.

Checking in with yourself

As we struggle with self-awareness, executive functioning and thinking extremely quickly, we can memorise all the lists of needs we like, but if we forget to use them, this might not be very helpful!

To overcome this, I've put structures in place to help create space between a request and my response. I try to check in with myself on whether I genuinely want to do it or whether I 'feel bad'.

This involves weighing up the pros and cons and thinking of other considerations. Do I have the *time* to do this activity? What will it be costing me – the 'opportunity cost' of doing this activity? If it's accepting a dinner invitation on a Thursday night, for example, does this mean that I will be exhausted on Friday? What are all the potential costs – how much could this dinner cost me in terms of money? Can I afford it? Is my body giving me any signs of resistance, such as my neck tensing up or jaw clenching? Where is the motivation coming from to say yes? What is the worst-case scenario if I say no?

I try to think through how this will impact me in the future, which definitely doesn't come naturally! However, I have never, ever regretted taking my time to answer, as unnatural as it might feel.

Instead of automatically saying yes, I try to think through my options, which has become a lot easier over time, as in 'I is for Impulsivity'. When we think so quickly, we can struggle with considering these different options, such as seeing a person on a different day instead. It can be difficult to think through a compromise, instead of just saying yes, especially if we feel pressure to make a decision (including if this is self-imposed pressure!).

This is why checking in with myself essentially means giving myself the time to think decisions through, as in 'E is for Executive Functioning'. Personally, I've tried to inject a new automatic answer to any requests of 'Can I let you know the answer to this later? I need to check my schedule'. I try to think of it like an automatic holding reply on emails if I'm away, instead of an automatic acceptance.

We are all entitled to the space and time to think about decisions. It doesn't make us 'bad' to sleep on big decisions – if anything, it makes us more respectful, as we're more likely to be able to uphold our commitment if we decide to say yes. Respecting our own needs is respecting those of other people too – we can't give from an empty cup.

Saying no

Saying no used to bring about terrible feelings of guilt and anxiety for me, and sometimes still does. I would happily prefer to be humiliated than stand up for myself in an awkward situation and be seen as 'difficult'. I felt like I needed to have a justifiable 'reason' to say no, such as saying that I was in a relationship if a stranger asked me on a date. I struggled with saying no to people who expected me to work for free, and even felt too guilty to ask for my bedroom back from a 'friend' who stayed in it whilst I went on holiday, meaning I had to find a new place to live!

Communicating our boundaries by saying no can be particularly difficult for people with ADHD who have Rejection Sensitive Dysphoria and tend to be highly empathetic. As we've maybe struggled a lot in our own lives, we might feel conflicted about potentially making somebody else feel the pain of being rejected (to the point that I've had entire romantic relationships with people I didn't like!) or want to prove ourselves.

No is a complete sentence. It is not rude or offensive to not want to do something.

It can be very useful to consider our beliefs about saying no, and the practical obstacles we come up against. For example:

→ What does saying 'no' feel like to you? What's stopped you from saying 'no' to requests you don't want to do in the past?

→ What things have you agreed to do for other people this week? How many of those things do you actually want to do?

→ How many requests have you said no to this week?

→ Do you often find that you don't have enough time to do all of the things you want to do for other people? Do you put these promises above time for yourself? What's the effect of this on you – do you have enough time for self-care?

→ When you've said no in the past, how have you done this? What happened as a result?

→ Can you identify a situation when you felt guilty for saying no, and imagine a pie chart of responsibility? What were the roles of the other people in this situation? There are rarely situations where all responsibility falls on us alone, even if that's just by other people communicating how they're feeling about a situation. You're not a mind reader!

After working with a therapist, I was given a task to practice, which was paying for something small with a £20 note without apologising for not having change.

I noticed how scared I was doing this exercise, and how tempting it was to apologise when asked if I had any change. I reminded myself that it was the cashier's job and not my responsibility to have the exact amount of change. This anxiety melted away when the cashier smiled and gave me the right amount of change, wishing me a good day.

If this resonates with you, you could try something similar by identifying a safe way to practise saying no. It could be something as simple as not replying to a message immediately (without apologising!), or leaving a party when you want to, instead of forcing yourself to stay until the end.

Communicating our boundaries

Sharing our boundaries explicitly to another person can be done verbally or in writing. Personally, I find it much easier to write down things that make me feel uncomfortable rather than speak them. It's important to remain neutral and be as clear as possible, such as saying, 'It's important to me that you… I'd like you to..'

It's also important to ask other people about their expectations of you before saying yes. It never hurts to ask for more information, so you can make the best-informed decision. This is particularly relevant to work situations, where we might jump to conclusions without having all of the facts, and automatically say yes.

Getting very specific on what is being asked of you, whether that's the deadlines for a project or exactly how many brownies you're expected to make for the bake sale, can be very helpful for ADHD-ers. It's even better if you can ask a person to send you this information in writing so you can refer back to it later on, which also gives you additional time to make a decision!

For ADHD-ers, another significant difficulty can be with remembering to check in with ourselves and to say no, if that's what feels right. Our brains can move so fast that we've completely forgotten the list of needs we read out that morning!

I've had plenty of experience with this, and some ways that have helped me include:

→ Having post-it notes on my laptop to remind me to 'wait before saying yes'.

→ Hiring a virtual assistant to be my 'gatekeeper', saying no to everybody who doesn't meet my boundaries. This is particularly helpful for work situations, as I'd always be working for free otherwise!

→ Identifying certain people who I tend to automatically say yes to the most and changing their name on my phone to remind me not to reply immediately!

→ Having phone backgrounds with questions such as 'How will saying yes to this feel in three weeks, three months, and three years?'

→ Using my calendar for *everything* in my life, including exercise classes and mealtimes!

Upholding your boundaries

Just because we communicate a boundary doesn't necessarily mean that it'll be respected. Sometimes we may have to restate our boundaries until they are properly listened to, especially if we've lived a life of people-pleasing! This can be difficult, but there is nothing wrong with saying no and standing up for yourself. Imagine if it was the other way around!

Once I started setting boundaries, I noticed how people would say yes and then immediately violate these boundaries. For example, I told someone I'd had relationship problems with that I didn't feel comfortable meeting them in person, but could have a phone call on the weekend. When we had the phone call, they said they happened to be in my area and suggested coffee! (I went and deeply regretted it – I'm definitely not perfect!)

This can be incredibly frustrating, especially for ADHD-ers who are prone to forgetting the boundaries we set due to our short-term memories.

If we notice our boundaries being violated after we've set them, the key thing is to reinforce them with action, such as saying no. For example, I could have said to the person who 'happened' to be in my area that I wasn't able to meet up with them, and the fact that they'd not respected my boundaries meant I needed more space before I felt able to continue speaking with them at all. This can feel very uncomfortable, but it's how we prove that we are serious about upholding our boundaries and respecting the limits we set for ourselves.

For ADHD-ers, this can be especially frustrating when it's already so difficult for us to identify and communicate a boundary. I've often found myself feeling so relieved at someone responding kindly at first that I let my guard down and impulsively say yes to anything they ask of me afterwards! It can also be very challenging for us to ask for help, as in 'B is for Burnout', and so holding people to what they've agreed to in terms of supporting us can be another uncomfortable situation.

To do this, it can be useful to express 'feeling' statements, such as saying 'When you do X, I feel Y. I'd prefer it if you did Z.' It's difficult for someone to argue with how you feel! You can also refer back to what you've already said and express how it makes you feel in that your boundaries aren't being respected.

It takes practice, but living a life with clear boundaries, where you're respected by the people in your life, leads to strong relationships, and overall happiness. There is literally nothing wrong with standing up for yourself, saying no and maintaining boundaries.

Ultimately, it's good for us to have a 'bottom line' for our boundaries, and to be able to identify when a situation isn't worth our time or energy. This could mean walking away, or setting new boundaries, such as only seeing certain people in specific situations. If you're struggling with this, reach out to somebody that you trust for help. It's your life – nobody else's!

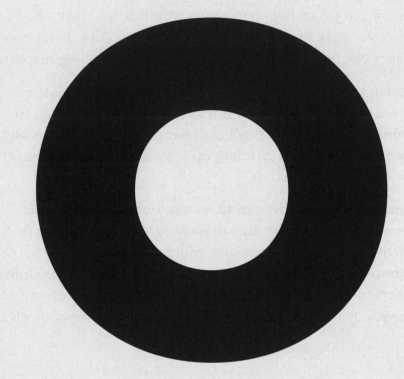

is for Organisation

Did you know?

- ADHD can cause serious issues with organisation, as this is what our prefrontal cortex (which is unregulated for ADHD-ers) is responsible for. There may also be sensory issues, as in 'Y is for Your Body', which can make us oblivious to 'mess'.

- Particularly when ADHD is undiagnosed and untreated, it has been said to contribute to problems succeeding in school, with successfully graduating and at work, lost productivity and reduced earning power, more accidents whilst driving and problems with the law (ADHD Awareness Month, 2020).

- A 2017 survey of 800 teachers found that 55 per cent reported concerns about possible undiagnosed ADHD in their students. Seventy-four per cent of these teachers did not know that learners with ADHD have difficulties in organisation and planning (Comres, 2017).

Organisation utilises our executive functioning skills, which ADHD-ers can struggle with, as in 'E is for Executive Functioning'. The prefrontal cortex, the part of the brain that is responsible for making decisions, memory and detail, is affected by ADHD, which can make everything seem like organised chaos. Ironically, some people with ADHD may appear extremely organised, because of finding coping mechanisms throughout their life to help them manage this. Others may be the complete opposite!

Focusing your mind

Having ADHD can mean that your mind can feel quite jumbled up. Dates, times, details and facts can all become a mishmash as the focus of your attention rapidly changes from one thing to the next. This can become extremely frustrating for ADHD-ers and those around them, and result in anxiety about trying to communicate the chaos inside your mind to the outside world.

Everybody is different, but for me writing things out really helps. This is particularly beneficial in terms of work and having meetings, as I tend to panic when put on the spot. Writing agendas beforehand helps me to summarise what I want to say and, ironically, appear very organised!

Mindfulness and meditation can also be very helpful in terms of relaxing your mind to try to focus on one thing. If you have ADHD, you may find yourself overusing your brain in certain areas and underusing it in others, so it is good to try to balance out the energy across the whole of the mind. If you imagine your brain as a television with all 15 channels playing at once, it can feel virtually impossible to concentrate on only one of them – however, you *can* train your brain to do so. It requires sustained mental effort and practice, but this is nature's remedy to overthinking. You just need to give your brain a rest.

Help yourself out in doing this as much as possible by cutting out any unnecessary distractions. Focusing with ADHD can sometimes feel like you are trying to work on a computer with 2o tabs open, in a room with music playing loudly out of surround-sound speakers, your phone flashing with notifications beside you, the television blaring and with a small herd of animals and children continuously running through the door. The great news is that you can literally and metaphorically remove the unnecessary tabs, turn off the music and television, put your phone on aeroplane mode and lock the door.

If you have ADHD, you might have ten different to-do lists and journals (at least!), or none at all. The secret to organising your mind is to make it simple. This means as few lists as possible. Although they can be extremely helpful, having lists upon lists and piles of journals to keep track of will have the opposite effect in terms of productivity. The ideal scenario is one journal for 'home' and one for 'work'. The home journal should contain a list of all your various administrative accounts and any to-do lists related to your personal life, diary entries, important dates to remember and so on. The work journal should contain information you would be okay with a colleague seeing – to-do lists relating to work, for example. I find it helpful to write a to-do list every morning so that my day is focused – even better to use is a whiteboard, so that you can be regularly reminded of your priorities in a visual way.

With to-do lists, a good technique is to only have three things on it at a time. If you can get a portable whiteboard, it's helpful to prioritise your day by dividing it into three sections: 'important but not urgent', 'urgent and important', 'not urgent and not important'. The 'urgent and important' things are your focus to get done first. The 'not urgent and not important' part you can fill with any thoughts that pop up throughout the day, which could otherwise be distracting. Even if you're not working, it can be helpful to plan your days this way, as it can be difficult to know how to organise our free time.

When it come to the tasks themselves, it's good to separate each one into manageable chunks. The key is making every task as basic and manageable as possible, and giving yourself more time than you think you will need. We will discuss more about this in 'T is for Time Management', but it's a good idea to set yourself a timer for each task and to take regular breaks.

Tips

- Reduce the number of distractions around you. Figure out what they are and how you can overcome them – see 'J is for Jobs' for how to avoid work distractions.

- Try to reduce the amount of time you spend on your phone. You can keep track of your screen time, charge it in a different room to the one that you sleep in or put it in a specific place throughout the day when focusing on other things.

- Have a routine each day that you can do on autopilot – for example, eating the same breakfast each morning.

- Recognise when you have the most energy in the day and prioritise your focus according to this.

- Tackle the tasks that you least want to do first in the day – think of your willpower like a battery that recharges when you sleep!

- Set yourself a timer (25 minutes has been proven to be optimal) of focus time, with five-minute break periods (University of Illinois at Urbana-Champaign,

2011). It's helpful to have a clock or stop-watch to do this, because using our phones can often lead to being distracted by other things!

▸ Prioritise tasks into 'urgent but not important', 'important but not urgent' and 'urgent and important'. Focus on the latter first, and break tasks down into separate steps of what you need to do.

▸ Give yourself longer than you think you will need.

▸ Set yourself one to-do list per day, focusing on three things at a time only. You could write these three things on a post-it note or whiteboard.

▸ Try the grounding techniques in 'G is for Grounding', such as meditation, to signal to your brain that it is time to focus.

▸ Ensure that your diet is healthy and balanced, and that you incorporate mealtimes and proper breaks into your day.

Improving your memory

Having ADHD can mean that our memories are impaired, as in 'E is for Executive Functioning'. This means we can we find ourselves constantly forgetting belongings, dates, appointments, names and so on, which can lead to a very disorganised life.

This can place a strain on interpersonal relationships, as in 'L is for Love'. People may equate forgetfulness with rudeness or simply not caring about them – such as forgetting birthdays!

This can also be problematic in terms of work, as seen in 'J is for Jobs'. Our work may expect us to be able to remember our various passwords to different systems or remember the different sign-off processes involved for different projects. Details are often very important when it comes to work – time is money. Spending an hour trying to remember your password, being locked out of your account and having to see IT to get back in is an hour of work missed.

The good news is that it is possible to hack your memory. You can remind yourself of what you need to remember and prepare in advance.

Tips

▸ Did your parents ever tell you to 'pack your school bag the night before?' Apply this to your adult life – prepare for tomorrow, today, such as by choosing your outfit.

▸ Have a phone charger on you at all times, including one specifically for your workplace.

▸ Write yourself a list of the things you need to check before leaving the house and stick it on the door. Make sure it is simple, short and attention-grabbing!

▸ Put a large keyring on your keys, such as a handkerchief.

▸ For things that you are at high risk of losing such as ID cards or glasses, hook them onto necklaces, chains or elastic bands. I have a hairband on my

printer card and automatically pop it onto my wrist
after using it instead of leaving it by the printer!

▸ Have a dedicated spot, such as a bowl, for your keys,
wallet and anything else that you are prone to losing
in your house. Make it an automatic part of your
routine to place these items in their home so that
you know where they are at all times.

▸ Set yourself calendar reminders on your phone or
computer for appointments – the day before and the
hour before! Make it a habit to check your calendar
every day.

▸ Make an effort to listen to people when they talk.
Maintain eye contact and focus on what they are
saying rather than thinking about what to say next.

▸ Post yourself visual reminders of things to remember
where you will see them.

▸ Give a spare set of keys to somebody you trust
who lives nearby so that you never have to call the
locksmith again!

▸ Have a chart to fill in when you have done
something, or take a photograph on your phone,
such as when taking your medication, so that you
know that you have done it.

▸ Write all of your passwords and various account
details in one journal that is easy for you to access,
but which is well hidden in your house. Try to reduce
the number of email accounts that you use to

one, and do a 'subscription inventory', as in 'F is for Finance', taking away all those that you do not need.

▶ When you are in control of deadlines, give yourself far more time than you need. When you are given a deadline, make a new, shorter deadline for yourself so that it feels more urgent. More on this can be seen in 'T is for Time Management'.

Organising your space

The chaos in the mind of a person with ADHD can sometimes find its way into their outside world, often resulting in a physical mess. Again, this is difficult not only for those with ADHD to find their belongings and feel a sense of calm, but also for those around them. For example, living in a shared house can be problematic if one person has a different understanding of what mess is to the others.

Before starting to take my medication, I was oblivious to mess. I was focused on the overall tidiness at a glance – swooping all of the mess in the cupboard or underneath the bed, as opposed to noticing the crumbs, hair and dust steadily piling up. I didn't understand the difference between folding a shirt into a general square shape and folding it properly. This caused many issues in my relationships with other people, as we had very different understandings of what my making an effort to clean looked like!

Learning how to see the mess is the first step for organising your space. Making a cleaning routine allows you to keep on top of the mess that builds up over the course of a week, which is especially helpful if you live with others. Putting a cleaning routine somewhere you will see it is helpful, such as the fridge, along with reminders on your phone.

Living in a messy environment can sometimes be a result of things building up that we don't need. As seen in 'F is for Finance', ADHD-ers can be prone to impulsive spending, which can result in the accumulation of lots of physical objects. Regular routines of sorting through your belongings to either sell or give away the things that you do not need are very helpful. A good test when you do this is to assess how often you have used the object – if it isn't within the last year, lose it. This can also be applied to more perishable goods, such as a weekly clean out of your fridge.

I'd strongly recommend 'ADHD-proofing' your environment by making it as easy as possible to clean. For example, I have washing baskets in every room to swoop objects into easily when I need to, and water bottles in every room so I don't bring cups in!

Tips

▶ Identify what the benefits are to you of living in a clean environment. Although we can all focus more with less distractions around us, you might have particular benefits from cleaning. For example, if you have a 'floordrobe' but love fashion, can you motivate yourself to treat your clothes with a little more kindness by hanging them up? Or would a cleaner kitchen enable you to cook more? Visualise the personal benefits of having a clean space to live in.

- Have a cleaning routine and stick to it. Ask somebody to help you identify what tasks need to be done in your living area and for any advice on cleaning products – they will likely be very happy to help!

- Invest in proper cleaning products to clean your space with, which will motivate you to do the job properly. Read the instructions of how to use and maintain these products, such as how to replace hoover bags. I recently invested in a robot vacuum cleaner which moves around by itself, which has been life-changing!

- Build daily cleaning into your routine, as in 'G is for Grounding'. For example, set yourself five minutes per day to clean as much of your room as possible, or ensure that you make your bed every morning. Set yourself small, achievable goals to build into your daily life.

- Schedule regular clear-outs and don't be afraid to get rid of the belongings that you don't use.

- Build 'homes' for your belongings. For example, paper trays for bits of paper, a key hook for your keys, a cutlery drawer and so on. If everything has its own place, you will be able to return it easily.

- Have a 'back-up' cupboard filled with emergency stashes of things you might run out of, such as toilet roll, and ensure this is always fully stocked.

- Buy food that can be stored for a long time, such as pre-chopped garlic, ginger and onions. Cooking big batches of food and freezing meals can be extremely useful!

▸ Make cleaning fun! Play your favourite music and dance around as you clean.

▸ When cleaning, try to organise your belongings into different categories. For example, putting clothes in one area of your room and papers in another. This helps us to group things together into manageable 'hills' rather than feel overwhelmed at a mountain of tidying. If you need an extra boost of motivation, talk to an ADHD coach or have an accountability buddy. One of my clients completely transformed her house by sending me before and after photographs each time she cleaned, which got her into the habit!

Organising your 'life administration'

As in 'G is for Grounding', routine and structure are very important for managing ADHD symptoms. They are the framework off which you can live your life, the things that should be done on autopilot so that you can use your brain for the things you want to focus on instead of worrying about small things throughout the day.

When it comes to life admin, there are a few different concepts that ADHD-ers can struggle with. These tend to be in the form of paperwork, bills, tax returns, doctor's appointments and so on – anything that is a bit difficult to wrap your head around quickly. Leaving these things to the last minute, or avoiding them altogether, is a recipe for disaster. Not only do you spend a lot of time worrying about them, even on a subconscious level, but it also tends to always be more stressful and worse if you leave things until the last minute.

Establishing a routine for life admin will improve your life dramatically. Sorting out these things as they happen, rather than when you seriously have to, will result in far less stress. They can seem extremely overwhelming, and therefore our brains tend to run away from them altogether (perpetuating the cycle of not being 'normal' and able to cope with routine activities), but when we actually get down to it, they can be quite straightforward. There are also people available to help you, even more so if you leave enough time to do them.

There are a few steps to getting on top of life admin:

1. Make a list of all of the life admin tasks that you know that you will need to acknowledge at some point in the next year. For example:

   • tax return

   • paying bills

   • paying rent/mortgage payments

   • doctor's check-ups

   • dentist check-ups

   • haircuts

   • eye tests.

2. Put a date next to each task that you have identified. Dedicate one hour to arranging all the appointments you

have identified. Now set yourself calendar reminders – for a month, week and day before, and on the day itself.

3. Take the time to set up a direct debit for the bills that need paying. Dedicate some time to figuring out how much each bill costs you and a budget, as in 'F is for Finance'.

4. Make a system for tackling life admin as soon as it arises. For example, when you receive a letter, put it in a specific place, such as a letter holder on your table. Dedicate a certain amount of time each weekend to life admin and going through these tasks that minute instead of putting them off any longer.

5. If the process of dealing with the life admin becomes stressful and overwhelming (such as being put on hold for a long period of time), engage in a mindfulness break as in 'Z is for Zen'. Don't be afraid to ask for help from the people around you – these things are tricky for everyone!

6. When you need to focus, consider asking a friend if they want to do a 'focus session' with you. You can either sit together or do this remotely, but dedicate a set amount of time to completing one of these tasks where you both can hold each other accountable – it is very effective! There are also online ways of doing this, such as Focusmate, which will connect you with a virtual co-worker as a 'body double'. I also sometimes do this with my clients as an ADHD coach!

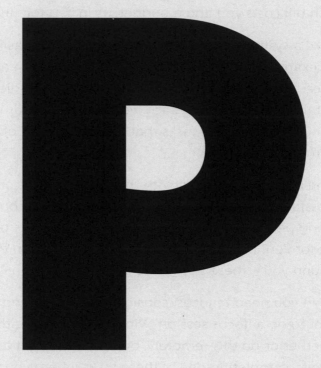

is for Procrastination

Did you know?

- It can be very difficult to concentrate on and finish tasks for people with ADHD, who are very prone to distraction and procrastination.

- Research published in 2018 found that 75 per cent of individuals with ADHD were classified as 'chronic procrastinators', confirming that procrastination is a pervasive issue for ADHD-ers (Pychyl, 2018).

- As in 'T is for Time Management', ADHD causes impairments in relation to our sense of time – so organisational problems could be addressed by externally stimulating our brains when a project needs completing.

The short attention span and impacted executive functioning associated with ADHD can contribute to issues with self-motivation. This underlies the overwhelming feeling at the thought of filling out a form, making an appointment or following a process. Our brains like to skip straight to the finish line, as quickly as possible – or not at all. We tend to encounter many distractions along the way that lead us to procrastinate – where we delay or postpone actions that need doing.

Whilst it might be very easy for a person with ADHD to set up a company overnight, it could be virtually impossible for them to do their washing. This is incredibly frustrating as we understand that we *have* the energy – we just don't seem to be able to choose what we focus our attention on.

When our mind is not wanting to focus on the thing we are trying to do, we are prone to procrastination – being distracted. It can feel like somebody else has the television remote to your focus, changing channels despite us trying our best to focus on one thing.

I find myself procrastinating by endlessly scrolling through social media, cleaning, talking to friends, watching television, writing – anything except what I am supposed to be doing. Focusing our mind takes up an intense amount of mental energy, as seen in 'O is for Organisation', and can exhaust us. But there are many ways that you can train yourself to stop procrastinating and start focusing.

Control your use of social media

I've written a whole book about how to overcome the addictiveness of social media, *The Reality Manifesto* (Maskell, 2022). So many of my clients struggle with using social media healthily, as it's deliberately designed to target the dopamine reward centres in our brains that are already impacted by ADHD! It is a procrastination paradise, filled with lots of short, surface-level content that is novel and fun, which has *literally* been designed to distract us, to grab and keep our attention, a valuable commodity. The issue is that we are often not actively choosing to spend our attention in this way, but rather become distracted by cute animal videos when going to check an email, for example. The satisfaction of opening a notification bubble gives us a little hit of dopamine, of feeling like we've 'completed' a task, instead of the one we actually intended to complete. Although we can chase this easy high all day long, it is the equivalent of binging on junk food for our minds.

This is because the highs are accompanied by lows. It is fraught with comparisons to others and an overload of unnecessary information, overwhelming our brains. We simply do not need to know what our friends ate for breakfast or how the weather is on the other side of the world. As a virtual rabbit hole in which we can feed our insecurities by searching for lives to compare our own to, it can be terrible for our self-esteem. It can help us to avoid our own feelings by providing an easy source of distraction, leaving us feeling numb.

Whilst there are certain benefits to social media, such as connections with others, it is best for us to choose when we want to use it – rather than be drawn into using it when we should be doing something else. With so many different notifications and lives to keep track of on one device, it is naturally bound to fragment our attention into lots of little pieces.

I have always asked friends to change my passwords to my social media accounts when I have needed to focus during significant periods of my life, such as for the month before any exams, which was always very effective. Deleting some accounts completely has also been very helpful in terms of removing addictive distractions that were only making me feel negative, such as Facebook.

There are various ways of controlling how you use social media, rather than being controlled by it:

→ **Assess how much you use social media.** You can look at your 'screen time' if your phone has this feature – the number of hours that you spend scrolling might shock you!

→ **Make an overall assessment of your social media habit.** Notice how you feel after going on it, who you follow, what your purposes in using it are. How does the thought of not being able to use it for a day make you feel? If it is anxious and worried, that is a good signal that you need a break.

→ **Clean up your accounts.** Choose to only follow people who make you feel happy and bring good-quality content into your life. Don't feel bad about unfollowing – see 'N is for No' for more on people-pleasing. If you don't want to unfollow your friends but their content makes you feel negative, you could mute them.

→ **Decrease the amount of time you mindlessly spend scrolling on social media.** There are a variety of options available to you:

- Allow yourself a certain time during the day in which you can go on social media and stick to it!

- Delete the apps from your phone. They tend to be much less addictive on computers!

- Deactivate your accounts. This will usually hold your information until you reactivate again in the future.

- Delete your accounts altogether, which should remove your information permanently.

- Ask a friend to change your passwords for you.

- Use apps such as Freedom, which can block certain software and websites on your computer for a specified time.

- Charge your phone in a different room to the one you

sleep in. Try not to use it when you don't need it, and try to get your most important task of the day done before checking it!

- Turn the colour off on your phone by setting it to black-and-white mode. This instantly makes it much less addictive and reduces the dopamine highs associated with bright colours such as red bubble notifications!

- See if any of your friends want to do a social media cleanse together. It can be helpful to be kept accountable!

Remove all distractions

Our focus is greatly improved by removing distractions, especially as it takes the average person over 23 minutes to regain their focus after being interrupted by distractions (Solis, 2019). By distractions, I mean anything that draws your attention away from the task you want to focus on – such as other people, emails or sounds such as the radio.

Your own mind might be the distraction. Try to simply notice every time that your mind wanders from what you are trying to do and bring it back to the present moment – without beating yourself up for it! Meditating on your breath is also a good way to gain control of your thoughts and learn how to focus sustained attention on one thing, in addition to clearing your mind. It can also be useful to have a notepad next to you to jot down any thoughts that pop up when you're trying to concentrate on something else.

If your workplace is distracting – for example, with people often coming to speak to you, or emails popping up

– consider asking your employer for reasonable adjustments for your ADHD. This doesn't necessarily have to involve talking about your ADHD, but it could be as simple as asking to move to a quieter part of the office so that you can work in peace, or asking for a work-from-home day once a week.

It is also helpful to put 'focus' slots into your diary so that if you have a shared calendar, other people can see that you are not to be disturbed during that time. You can put an automatic reply 'out of office' message on your emails and dedicate a certain portion of the day to different focuses.

Body doubling can also be very useful for this, with websites such as Focusmate enabling you to be connected with someone else who wants to concentrate on something! By telling somebody else what you intend to do during this time, you become accountable to them. This is how ADHD coaching works too – we usually set goals and actions between each session, setting out exactly when and how you plan to do these things! I've had many 'implementation sessions' with clients where they've just needed someone to help them stay on track with certain tasks they really don't want to do, like taxes!

Understand yourself

We all tend to have different bouts of energy throughout the day. Some people may work best in the morning whilst others may be extremely productive at night. ADHD is commonly associated with sleep problems, as in 'S is for Sleep', where we may feel hyperactive and productive!

We may also learn and focus best in a particular way, which

may be important to understand about yourself if you have ADHD and struggle with 'conventional' methods of learning. For example, I can focus by writing things down, whereas a friend of mine learns by walking around and reading things out loud. You could learn by physically 'doing' things or making connections between certain concepts. I connected the case law names in my degree to fictional stories that I made up to relate to the facts which always helped me to remember them, though that might sound like an extra layer of complication to anybody else. I also used to read my notes whilst working out in the gym!

Diet can also impact our ability to focus, as can medication and exercise. To focus on something for a sustained period, we want to avoid short bursts of energy followed by depletion, which means avoiding sugar and caffeine as in 'M is for Medication'.

To understand how you focus best:

1. Think about when you have been able to focus successfully in the past. What enabled you to focus so well – how did you learn? Try to remember as much as you can and write it down in a list.

> For example, I've been able to focus best when writing things down, when I've had no other distractions around me and no social media accounts active! I found making up stories connected to what I needed to remember very fun, and even turned it into a song so I could sing this (internally!) during my exams.

2. Consider activities that you do and do not enjoy doing. What is the reason that you find something 'boring' or 'fun'?

> I find being creative fun and using my imagination to write books (like this one!). I find situations that limit my creativity to be very boring, like having to fill in forms in a precise way.

3. Think about how you can apply your own focus technique to boring activities, and anything that you might have to do to prepare for this.

> I could make the forms more interesting to fill out by doing them immediately before a fun activity such as a trapeze class, or going to do them in a new environment, such as a local coffee shop. I could also look for ways the forms could be improved and maybe send this along as feedback!

Timing

As in 'T is for Time Management', timing is ultimately key to managing our ADHD and planning out our lives accordingly. It is when we run out of time, or think we don't have enough, that we rush and make mistakes.

ADHD-ers also react well to timelines, pressure and deadlines. They tend to not react so well to stress, so it is a good idea to always leave as much time as possible. If you can start something now instead of in six weeks, start it now. Become ultra-organised and set your own deadlines to motivate yourself. Break down a task into different parts and set yourself a deadline for each of these, scheduling these out in your calendar. With enough time to complete it and broken down into chunks, the overwhelming mountain of a task will become an easy, manageable part of your day.

It is also good to train your focus using timing. The Pomodoro technique has been proven to increase productivity, by setting a timer for 25 minutes in which to focus and taking a five-minute break. Like high-intensity interval training, but for your mind. The concept can be adjusted to whatever task you are trying to get done – for example, setting a timer for five minutes to do the washing up. Self-motivation is simply *forcing* yourself to do something and engaging those executive functions.

Done is better than perfect

Instead of 'perfect', aim for done. Once something is done, then you can perfect it – if you want to! 'K is for Kindness' explains how we can be kind to ourselves and gently support ourselves through doing something tricky. By speaking to yourself negatively when you procrastinate, you are perpetuating a cycle of anxiety and self-hatred that will keep you in the same place instead of actually getting anything done at all.

Trying something is the only way you will improve at it – nobody starts out perfect. We are all human, and nobody is born good at everything. Skills come from practice and sustained effort, which can be done by anyone – whether they have ADHD or not.

Having ADHD does not mean that you are doomed to never be good enough at anything. It doesn't mean that you should just give up before even trying – on the contrary, ADHD can be seen as a 'superpower', as in 'W is for Weaknesses'. It enables you to think differently to neurotypical people, with more energy than most, which you can translate into incredible achievements. Once you understand how to manage over-active thoughts, you can choose to dedicate the immense power of your brain to anything you want to focus on.

is for Quitting

Did you know?

- People with ADHD have been reported to be more likely to quit a job because of dislike than those without (Kuriyan *et al.*, 2013).

- A study found that 32.2 per cent of students with the combined type of ADHD drop out of high school, compared to 15 per cent of teenagers with no psychiatric disorder (Breslau *et al.*, 2011).

- Research has suggested that university students with ADHD in the UK do not receive enough support, finding it is usually limited to that which would be provided for students with dyslexia, which can result in them dropping out (Attention UK, n.d.).

As ADHD-ers, we tend to be impulsive and have short attention spans. We may commonly find ourselves in situations where we start new projects regularly and energetically but can't keep up this level of determination and quit. The quitting tends to feed into the cycle of low self-esteem and feeling 'not good enough', resulting in impacted relationships with others and general exhaustion.

I used to live in fear of starting anything because I didn't trust myself to finish anything. It was very frustrating being unable to control which new ideas I would put into life on any given day, before getting bored of them a week later. Living in this way perpetuates the short attention span and limiting beliefs of not being able to finish anything we start that can accompany ADHD. 'I is for Impulsivity' discusses how to train your brain to overcome these difficulties and establish a structure in place, but it's important to remember that you aren't bound to anything forever.

When to quit

If something is making you more unhappy than happy, then you should certainly quit. However, ADHD-ers can tend to quit things as easily as we start them, which can often be impulsive, emotional decisions that we might regret. The key to this, again, is patience, as in 'T is for Time Management' – thinking over our decisions properly, including whether to start or quit something.

You do not have to quit something the moment you are unhappy or feel overwhelmed with emotion, as in 'R is for Rejection'. You can wait it through and grow your resilience muscle, testing yourself and growing as a person, proving to yourself that you can *choose* to quit something rather than have it all happen before you even know what is going on.

Having ADHD can be extremely emotionally overwhelming. The best thing to do when you feel overwhelmed is to remove yourself from the situation, be kind to yourself and rest. Taking a break from a stressful situation will give you the literal and metaphorical space to think things through and process your feelings.

It is good to examine your feelings about quitting in the same way as you would when starting something. Look at it from all angles and consider the impact it will have on you long-term – on your finances, overall happiness levels and life.

Try to think about the alternatives – what would the benefits of not quitting be?

When you are feeling overwhelmed, it can be hard to imagine feeling any differently about a situation, but a good rule of thumb is to give it at least a week.

However, if a situation is causing you significant stress or putting you in danger, then leave. You should be able to weigh up whether something is seriously harming you or just stressing you out. Difficult experiences can lead to growth, but putting yourself through significant harm or in danger is never a good idea – always leave as soon as possible in this situation. You do not owe anybody anything in terms of being exploited.

Similarly, weigh up the pros and cons of a situation. Staying in a job for a year can have different benefits to, say, staying in a negative hobby. For example, I joined a professional cheerleading club and hated it, but felt too guilty to quit, having convinced a friend to join with me and committed to a competition. Instead of leaving, I moaned to my friend and half-heartedly attended sessions on sufferance for months, until quitting just before the competition out of anxiety that I would ruin it for the whole team! It's good to see your time as money – if one reason for continuing something you don't enjoy is because you've invested into it, you are simply wasting more of your time and money.

By quitting, you are ultimately taking responsibility for your own happiness. You can't look to other people to give you permission to leave or create excuses so that you can go – you just need to accept that you don't want to do it anymore and go. It's like ripping off a plaster in that it can be awkward and painful at the time but is over before you know it. Everyone tends to be much more grateful when you just quit something that you really do not want to do, because you aren't wasting anybody's time.

How to quit

We may feel a lot of shame over quitting things. ADHD-ers tend to overthink a lot and can find ourselves catastrophising the 'quitting' process far beyond what it needs to be, replaying previous experiences of failure over in our heads. However, if you choose to quit and are sure it's the right decision for you, the world won't end. Life goes on, and it's better to leave a bad situation than to stay in one whilst being miserable. At the end of the day, it's your life!

This being said, it's obviously good to think things through as much as you're able to, to ensure that it's not an impulsive action that you might later regret. For example, walking out on a job because you've argued with a colleague would only impact you negatively, and might make it difficult to get a good reference in the future.

In contrast, if you can consider this as part of your overall feelings about your workplace, with the understanding that some days are better than others in all jobs, but still reach the conclusion that it's not the right place for you, there's nothing stopping you from leaving when you're ready. Quitting in a calm, respectful and upfront way is likely to result in your employer supporting you however they can – they probably don't expect you to stay there forever!

This ultimately requires us to use our brain tools discussed in 'E is for Executive Functioning' of managing our emotions, to think things through fully, and not to act impulsively.

How to quit something

→ **When you feel ready to quit something, give yourself a week.** Allow yourself an additional week of knowing you are planning to quit, but don't tell anyone during that time. If you still want to quit at the end of the week, go ahead and proceed. Try to imagine how you will feel about the situation in six months' and one year's time.

→ **Try to only tell a select few people that you trust,** ideally outside of the situation.

→ **Consider alternatives.** For example, if you want to quit a job because of difficulty with your ADHD symptoms, consider disclosing your ADHD to your employer, as in 'J is for Jobs', so that they can make reasonable accommodations for you.

→ **Behave appropriately and respectfully.** This will usually mean being as communicative and upfront as possible – for example, by ending a relationship face to face.

→ **Be honest.** Do not overly apologise or appropriate more blame to yourself than you have to, but stand your ground and explain your reasoning clearly.

→ **Make this as easy as possible for yourself.** Things that could help include speaking about the situation first to someone you trust, who can help you to quit, or writing down the reasons you want to quit so you have them to hand in case you feel overwhelmed.

→ **Offer to complete any existing obligations to the people involved.** This could be working out your notice period or finding someone to replace you in a rental agreement, for example.

Maintain your boundaries – if you want to quit and someone is not accepting this, remember that you have every right to quit and no one deserves to make you feel otherwise, as in 'N is for No'. Do not let people guilt you into doing something you don't want to do – especially if this is harming you. Don't be afraid to uphold your boundaries with action, such as by contacting the police if someone is repeatedly messaging you when you've asked them not to.

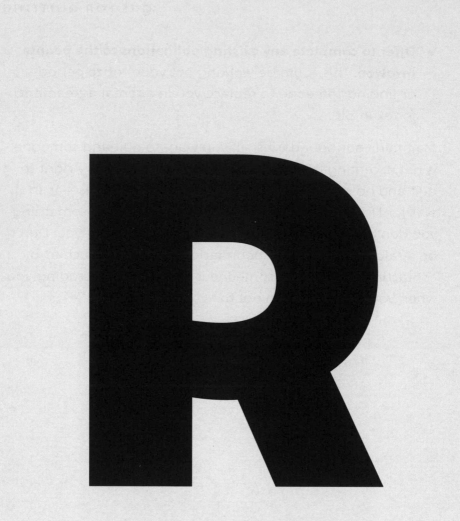

is for Rejection

Did you know?

- Dr William Dodson coined the phrase 'Rejection Sensitive Dysphoria' (RSD), finding that it appears to be the one emotional condition that is found only with ADHD. This can result in a person being triggered to feel extreme pain by real or perceived rejection, is said to be genetic and neurological, and lasts for very short periods of time (Dodson, 2016).

- If this emotional response is internalised, it can appear as a severe mood swing, such as suddenly feeling extremely depressed. If it is externalised, it can manifest as rage at another person or situation – 50 per cent of people who are court mandated for anger management treatment have previously unrecognised ADHD (Dodson, 2016).

- It has been reported that nearly one in three people with ADHD say that RSD is the hardest part of living with ADHD (Bhandari, 2o2o).

Rejection Sensitive Dysphoria (RSD) is commonly linked to ADHD (despite not being officially 'medically' recognised or part of the DSM criteria), and, for me, it's the hardest part about having ADHD. This refers to the extreme emotional sensitivity and pain that a person with RSD may feel when triggered by the perception of being rejected. Whilst nobody likes being rejected, this is the one emotional symptom that has only been associated with ADHD as opposed to other conditions. Dr William Dodson says it is genetic and neurological, but it may also come from people with ADHD being typecast as 'lazy' or a failure in the past. RSD can be expressed outwards in intense bursts of rage and impulsive decision making, or internalised by a person, causing them to feel so overwhelmed that they may even feel suicidal. When I speak to people about RSD, it can feel as though it's not always taken seriously, but it can have a seriously devastating impact on all areas of our lives, from our self-esteem to relationships. As an ADHD coach, RSD shows up consistently in every single client I have, significantly impacting their life. However, it is something we can work on managing, once we understand it!

For me, it feels like an overwhelming rush of emotion that overloads my system so much that I just want to turn it off in any way that I can. When I calm down, the feelings go away very quickly, but it can be very scary and upsetting to experience, especially when I didn't know about RSD and why this was happening.

The tidal wave of emotions literally taking over my body can feel like the worst feeling in the world, as though I lack control over my mind, almost like an emotional panic attack. Before I was diagnosed, this happened so often that I was convinced I'd be sectioned if I explained it to anybody in full. I could feel seriously suicidal one night and wake up completely fine the next morning, almost feeling like I was gaslighting myself and beating myself up for being emotional, when I really needed help.

Learning about RSD, especially the fact that it has been proven by researchers to exist and to have the effects I was experiencing, changed everything for me. Now I can recognise it and take action to deal with it appropriately, without becoming scared, which only makes things worse!

RSD can result in us experiencing severe social anxiety, constantly trying to anticipate what everyone around us wants, searching for guidance in others instead of living our own life. We may become obsessed with keeping the overwhelming feelings at bay by taking responsibility for the feelings of others, in the hope of not being rejected, as in 'N is for No'.

It can also result in depression. People with RSD may simply stop trying to do anything, failing to see the point in applying for a job or seeing people they care about, because of the exposure to potential rejection. We may be chronic underachievers as a result and be consistently unhappy, anticipating rejection everywhere in life, seeing it as pointless as a result. This is what happened to me when I tried to figure out what job to do, as I was so overwhelmed.

Contrastingly, RSD could manifest as unrealistically high standards of perfection in some people. We might suffer from exactly the same utter lack of self-esteem, but mask it with punishing ourselves into overworking. We might believe that when we achieve X, we will 'deserve' happiness, but X might be virtually impossible to achieve. I've also definitely experienced a lot of this in my life, and still do, which is horrible because it impacts my ability to enjoy the things I work so hard to achieve – it's as though it just gets replaced with a higher standard. I've had coaching clients tell me of the dread they felt when their homework was handed around the class as the best practice to follow, because they were already feeling that they couldn't meet these same standards next time.

Another aspect of RSD is self-sabotage, as in 'Q is for Quitting'. It can unfortunately lead to impulsive, emotionally charged decisions that can make us feel guilty and embarrassed afterwards, blaming ourselves in a never-ending cycle, that ironically feels very lonely. We might quit jobs or hobbies because of our fear of rejection.

Our personal relations with others can suffer dramatically because of RSD. People-pleasing tends to often backfire or can result in toxic relationships being prioritised above those who genuinely care for us. Nobody will ever be able to convince us that they always like us, all the time, no matter how hard they try. I used to be constantly checking in with school friends to ask if they still liked me, which ironically may have put them off me! If this resonates, consider your patterns in relationships throughout your life – how many people have you lost along the way due to RSD?

As in 'L is for Love', romantic relationships can also be impacted significantly because of being hyper-sensitive to rejection. Our partners can be bewildered at our overreactions to small things, such as them taking a few hours to return a text or lateness. They may not understand why we think we are so difficult to love and, in the end, believe what we say – a self-fulfilling prophecy. Our anticipation of rejection can sadly lead us to self-sabotage good relationships with people who do genuinely care about us. Relationships that are overshadowed by feelings of anticipated rejection tend to be volatile and result in someone with RSD feeling that love is 'conditional'. The ironic cruelty of RSD is that the sufferer can often reject others in the hope of protecting themselves. Feelings of potential rejection can lead to dramatic, impulsive decisions such as quitting a job or cutting somebody out of our lives without thinking – sometimes in the ill-conceived hope of the other person showing that they care.

Having ADHD and RSD is incredibly lonely. It means you are struggling with all the symptoms of ADHD in this vacuum of loneliness, where you might believe that nobody truly cares about you. The symptoms bounce off each other – not being able to complete things due to insecurity that stems from previous failures and an inability to ask for help, exacerbated by perceived loneliness and rejecting everyone as a result.

RSD can also manifest physically. Our bodies might react to the perceived threat of rejection by becoming unwell, overly tired or hyperactive. Some people may shut off completely and find it very difficult to formulate words to express how they are feeling, which can be very frustrating for both them and the people around them. It is very difficult to treat RSD as it hits so quickly, and the emotions can overwhelm a person very suddenly. One second we might feel fine, and the next we could feel intensely despondent.

ADHD medication has helped me with RSD to the extent that I can think more clearly and slowly about my different options, rather than feeling one crushing wave of emotion. Having ADHD coaching has also helped me significantly in being able to examine what kinds of situations trigger my RSD, to question my thoughts and build up a stable life that can remain even if I'm rejected at times.

Ultimately, the key to dealing with rejection is to build up our self-esteem, so that it is not reliant on the acceptance of other people, just ourselves.

Reframing our thoughts

The perception of rejection can be so overwhelming that we act without thinking, when often there may not have even been any rejection in the first place! I would equate this to 'gaslighting' yourself, imagining scenarios that aren't really happening and driving yourself to act erratically.

This boils down to a lack of trust that others will like us for who we are. When we start liking ourselves, then we start to understand that we are pretty great as we are and do not need to 'do' anything for others to like us.

In addition to learning the art of patience and slowing down our thoughts, as in 'E is for Executive Functioning', we can also learn to interject rational thoughts amongst the hurricane of emotions. We have to train ourselves to trust other people to like us and for that to be our automatic thought, as opposed to searching for all the reasons that people wouldn't like us. This can be done by staying aware of our tendencies to perceive rejection and actively combatting any worries, and by reminding ourselves that we are liked and accepted.

Managing RSD

1. Think about a time you have experienced RSD previously and have been overwhelmed by your own emotions. What triggered the RSD, what was it like to experience and what helped it pass?

   For example, I have terrible RSD when applying for jobs and receiving any rejections. This shows up for me by believing that I'll never be able to get a job, crying and feeling as

> though the world is ending. Going to sleep usually helps me, as I tend to feel better in the morning!

2. Make a list of triggers, as in things that you may perceive as rejection from others. This could include anything from feeling excluded in social settings to somebody not replying to your messages for several hours.

> I can feel RSD if I'm not actively invited out with friends (as I don't want to invite myself), or if someone doesn't reply to a text message (especially if I see them active on social media!). I also feel it when I apply for jobs and have interviews.

3. Create a list of things that make you feel calm, happy and secure. These could include activities such as cooking, playing music, bubble baths, reading a book, having a massage, exercising, talking to a friend or writing, for example. When you are feeling overwhelmed, try to do one of these activities as soon as possible.

> Journaling, reading, watching movies or an addictive television show, painting, and so on!

4. Hack your life to reduce the number of triggers and increase the number and accessibility of things that make you feel secure. For example, if unresponsive communication styles trigger you, avoid dating people who have problems with communication. Or if doing yoga makes you feel secure, sign up to a gym or appoint a space that you can go and do yoga in when you are feeling triggered.

> I have my notifications switched off on my phone, mute friends' posts on social media so they don't show up automatically and try always to have a notebook nearby.

5. When you are feeling triggered, train your brain to look for the secure things first. If this happens a lot, maybe keep a list on you at all times. Do something that makes you feel secure, such as calling a friend, before doing anything else. Train this to be your automatic response. You could also ask yourself if this will matter in three weeks, three months and three years.

    > If I'm feeling as though friends don't want me to come out with them, I'll look for the evidence that proves they *do* – such as them talking about it in front of me, assuming that I'll come! I'll try to notice the thought and choose to believe the opposite.

6. If you are feeling overwhelmed by RSD, remind yourself that you are experiencing RSD as a result of your ADHD, which will soon pass. Try to leave any situations as soon as possible to calm down and be as kind as possible to yourself, doing one of your 'secure' activities. It's a good idea to try to distract yourself until the feelings have passed, such as by watching a film or reading a book.

    > I try to get to sleep as soon as possible whenever I'm feeling highly emotional!

7. If you're feeling overwhelmed by emotion and tempted to act upon it, try to question your thoughts. Try to imagine that you're a lawyer advising a client, and give yourself the validation that you're seeking in this way. For example, it can be helpful to write down answers to the below:

    -   What are the facts of what's happened? (No emotions or opinions, just the provable facts.)

For example, my client hasn't been invited to breakfast with their friends, which they've seen happening on social media.

- How has this made your client feel and react? What do they believe has happened, and why?

My client is extremely upset, and thinks they deliberately didn't invite her because they don't like her. She's now questioning all of their previous conversations and trying to find reasons about why they don't like her.

- Is this a reasonable or realistic explanation? Is there enough proof or evidence available for this? Are there any other possible explanations?

The friends live close to each other, so it's possible that they bumped into each other at the cafe. My client doesn't have concrete evidence proving that they don't like her – in fact, they often message her to say how much they care about her.

- What does your client want to do? What do they *really* want behind the emotion?

Right now, my client wants to cut them off as friends and never speak to them again, because she is so upset. Ultimately, she obviously cares about them and wants reassurance that she is liked by her friends, and to be included.

- What would you advise them to do? What's the best course of action for them in the long run?

I would advise her to do something else for a while such as a yoga class, get off social media and remind herself of all the proof that these people care about her. I'd suggest dropping them a message later on to ask if they want to meet up. She could mention that she saw the breakfast on social media and ask to join next time.

- Can you write your client a short letter, validating their experiences and giving them advice?

Dear Leanne, I know you feel very upset and left out by not being invited to the breakfast. However, there may be many reasons why this happened, and social media often shows us the highlights reels of other people's lives, with no explanation.

Your friends care about you very much, and it's unlikely that they'd deliberately try to make you feel left out – just look at all your messages from them! I know it must feel very distressing to have seen them meeting up and triggered your Rejection Sensitive Dysphoria, but if you can, I'd recommend doing a yoga class to relax and revisiting this later on.

I'd suggest messaging your friends after a good night's sleep to ask how their weekend was, and mention that you saw they'd met up. If you feel comfortable to do so, you could ask to join next time, and suggest another time for you all to have breakfast together.

You are very loved, and your experiences are valid. I know this feels very unfair, but try to let the feelings pass, and remind yourself of how loved you are.

8. Use a mood tracker app or journal to regularly record your feelings. Find all the opposite reasons to what your thoughts are telling you in relation to potential rejection from others. For example, if you think that someone doesn't like you, gather the proof that they do like you.

9. Don't undermine your feelings. It is completely normal

and appropriate to feel pain. Suffering is when we add pain for feeling pain.

There may be many situations in which you respond completely appropriately, but the point is to accept and allow your feelings to be there, instead of beating yourself up more. It can be helpful to reach out to someone you trust for support, and allow yourself space to process your emotions before acting on them.

Having RSD does not mean that there is anything wrong with you. It means that you feel things on a deeper level than most and, as a result, tend to be more compassionate. Understanding the stress and emotions that your body can experience in one go means that you tend to be good at understanding the stress of other people, as it arises in small manageable chunks!

Remember to be kind to yourself, no matter what. You are deserving of love, and the people around you will love you unconditionally, even if it doesn't always feel that way.

is for Sleep

Did you know?

- ADHD has been called a '24-hour disorder' by researchers (Weiss and McBride, 2018). Almost three out of four children and adolescents, and up to four out of five adults with ADHD have a sleep disorder. ADHD can affect our 'circadian rhythm' (sleep–wake cycle), potentially making it harder to fall asleep or causing disruptions throughout the night, making it difficult to wake up and function well throughout the day without falling asleep.

- A study has proved strong crossover between symptoms of ADHD and narcolepsy, such as excessive daytime sleepiness and inattention (Oosterloo *et al.*, 2006). The high symptom overlap suggests that both conditions could be misdiagnosed.

- Researchers have related ADHD to interest-based performance, finding that ADHD-ers can be at risk of falling asleep when they are bored, if their nervous system disengages. This can be very dangerous if it occurs at inappropriate times, such as when driving (Dodson, 2022).

ADHD-ers commonly encounter difficulty sleeping. Seventy-five per cent of adults with ADHD have been reported to experience insomnia (Dodson, 2022). Our minds might race with thoughts late at night or we might have more energy in the evening, making it difficult to get to sleep. If you take stimulant medication, this also can keep you awake throughout the night, making you feel wired. As a result, you are likely to be tired throughout the day. The general stress associated with ADHD can impact anybody's sleeping patterns!

ADHD symptoms tend to become a lot worse without enough sleep, and there's a lot of crossover between ADHD and sleep conditions such as narcolepsy, causing potential misdiagnosis. Executive functioning and self-motivation become much harder without the basic necessity of energy from having enough sleep. Sleep problems can manifest differently in different people and seem to become worse in ADHD-ers with age. Researchers have found that, before puberty, 10 to 15 per cent of children with ADHD have trouble falling asleep; by age 12-and-a-half this is 50 per cent, and by age 30, it's more than 70 per cent (Dodson, 2022).

Difficulty falling asleep

As ADHD-ers are known to have racing minds and find it hard to sit still, the thought of actually shutting down our bodies for sleep can seem impossible. This is even more the case if we have spent our days in a buzz of distraction or hyper-focus, ignoring any stresses that we might be feeling. The minute we lie down in the dark, the thoughts can all pour into our heads, and we can be hit with a sense of energy compelling us to 'do' something to avoid all these feelings. As in 'Y is for Your Body', we might also be oblivious to physical discomfort throughout the day which could manifest as pain when we go to sleep, such as poor posture whilst sitting.

The thing that many people 'do' is go on their phones – the phone is usually accessible and nearby, and it perfectly absorbs our attention. The link between screen time at night and greater problems related to sleep for adolescents with ADHD has been proven by research (Becker and Lienesch, 2018).

Having an evening routine, as in 'G is for Grounding', is very helpful in terms of falling asleep. This might involve turning screens off at least one hour before bed, time to de-compress after the day and avoiding any stimulants after a certain time, for example.

Restless sleep

ADHD brains might stay activated throughout the night, waking us up with incessant thinking about the things we need to do. We then face the problem of falling back asleep all over again! It may also be quite uncomfortable sleeping next to us if our physical hyperactivity remains throughout the night – for example, by tossing and turning. As in 'Y is for Your Body', physical symptoms can accompany ADHD such as 'restless leg syndrome' or a need to keep moving.

This impacts on the quality of our sleep and can cause us to feel tired the next day. One particularly annoying thing I experience is waking up in the night but being half asleep, so unable to move physically but inundated with thoughts and worries. This has been referred to as sleep paralysis. It's hard to tell how long it lasts, so even if it is only for a few minutes, I can wake up feeling as though I have had been awake all night.

This is especially worse for me if I am particularly hyper-focused on something or feeling stressed – I will often wake up in the night 'working' in my brain or wake myself up with thoughts about work!

It can be helpful to try out different options in terms of what can help with this. Meditation, as in 'Z is for Zen', can calm down our nervous system and routines that avoid stimulating our brains too much, such as reading a pleasant, non-addictive fiction book, are helpful. I also find weighted and electronic blankets to help, and 'falling back to sleep' meditations – but these do require going on my phone, so they require a lot of willpower not to go on anything else!

Difficulty waking up and staying awake

It can also be hard for ADHD-ers to wake up when they are supposed to. This may be because of the difficulty in managing to sleep, making us feel exhausted and reluctant to go through the entire process again. Our internal clock may not recognise the hours that we are 'supposed' to sleep and be awake, seeing it as another box of society to fit into. This cycle leads to ADHD-ers being exhausted throughout the day and with less energy than other people, when we tend to need a lot more to help regulate our brains in the same way.

We may also have trouble with staying awake. I used to regularly fall asleep in school classes despite not having particular problems with sleep at night. It has been suggested that if a person with ADHD doesn't have interest in an activity, their nervous system can disengage to a point that can induce sudden extreme drowsiness and falling asleep. We can literally fall asleep from being bored, which can be life-threatening if we happen to be driving (Dodson, 2022).

Improving the quality of our sleep can help with staying awake throughout the day. If you are affected by falling asleep at inappropriate times, then it is advisable not to drive or do anything that can be dangerous to do if you aren't fully awake, such as operating heavy machinery. In the UK, ADHD-ers have a duty to disclose their ADHD if it affects their ability to drive safely (Driver and Vehicle Licensing Agency, 2o2o).

Improving our sleep

The issue is ultimately difficulty relaxing and switching off. As we will see in 'Z is for Zen', there are a variety of ways that you can do this, but a good way to approach sleep generally is to apply the concepts we have used in this book. We need to make our goals realistic and achievable, and to be kind to ourselves. We need to reduce the overall stress and think about how we can 'hack' ourselves to actually truly want to sleep, how to reduce the pressure and expectations we put on ourselves. We need to stop thinking that there is something wrong with us or getting angry when we can't sleep, because this just heightens the emotional cycle of frustration.

To do this, we can look at our own specific sleep patterns and make a strategy:

1. Make an assessment of your sleeping patterns. Write down:

   - How many hours of sleep you typically get each night.

   - Any problems you have associated with getting to sleep, staying asleep or waking up.

   - What is behind these problems – for example, if your mind is racing, what are you generally thinking about?

- How tired you feel throughout the day.

- How stressed you are in general and why.

- What you equate to a good night's sleep. Think about the details – do you prefer to be hot or cold? Do you prefer to sleep alone or to have company? To go to sleep early or late? To have lights or sounds on or off?

2. Make a list of your barriers to a good night's sleep and try to think of solutions to these. For example:

    - Dislike being cold: use a hot water bottle or electric blanket.

    - Dislike being too hot: use a fan or invest in a lighter duvet.

    - Distracted by lights/sounds: use 'white noise' apps, earplugs or an eye mask.

    - Can't switch off thoughts: meditate before sleep, or listen to an audiobook. Avoid stimulants such as caffeine before bed.

    - Stressed out: find a therapist, as in 'M is for Medication'.

    - Going on your phone in the night: charge it in a different room.

    - Trouble waking up: invest in an alarm clock that suits your particular needs, such as one that runs around the room!

    - If there are any that you can't find a solution to, google them! There is a solution for every problem. Don't let your brain find excuses such as 'I can't afford X'.

Sleep should be your number-one priority – you won't be able to work as well without it!

3. Create a 'sleep routine' as in 'G is for Grounding', using your lists as the basis. Make yourself a routine including:

- What time you turn off your electronics each evening – screens, phones and so on.

- Where you will charge your electronics each night whilst you sleep (as far away as possible!).

- The things that you will do before bed, such as meditating, reading, writing or exercise.

- What time you will go to bed – try to make this the same each evening.

- What time you will wake up – as above, try to make this the same, even on the weekends.

Having a routine that you don't have to think about too much will allow you to do these things on autopilot and signal to your body that it is time to shut down. You are a human being designed for sleep – you are capable of sleeping peacefully for eight hours each night, you just need to train yourself to do it in the right way for you. Make sure that the routine is easy and achievable and be kind to yourself if you don't follow it one evening – just start again!

Tips

▶ Charge your phone in a different room. Phones are the number-one distraction for us and are so easy to go on in the night, scrolling for hours. It is also really unhealthy to scroll for hours first thing in the morning, stopping you from getting out of bed! Make it as difficult as possible to access your phone when you are supposed to be sleeping and don't let your mind think of excuses – you can buy an alarm clock or invest in a CD recording of meditations, for example. If you are truly unable to charge it in a different room, make sure it is on aeroplane mode at night! Nobody needs to contact you when you are asleep.

- I'd recommend avoiding sleep apps, such as those that track your sleep, or wearing smart watches to bed. Even if we enjoy seeing this information, it still has the inherent problem of making us within easy reach of a screen and notifications!

- Avoid screens, especially your phone, for at least one hour before bed each night. Our phones are perfect for engineering racing thoughts and overloading our brains with information that we simply do not need.

- Set a bedtime and stick to it for a week. Don't pressure yourself to sleep when you are in bed, just lie there and try to count or play games with yourself. Things that help me to get to sleep are listing every single thing that happened in my day factually (without stressing about it!), thinking of words in different categories from A to Z and counting the number of breaths I can do into my stomach.

- Try to do something before bed each evening that switches off your mind. This could be reading a book (make sure it's not too addictive!), writing, meditating or yoga, for example. Avoid television or watching something on a screen, because the light will affect your brain and may make it think it is still daytime.

▶ Invest in different things to promote a good night's sleep. I use an electric blanket, hot water bottle, weighted blanket, furry duvet covers and a sunlight emulating alarm clock. Some people may benefit from essential oil humidifiers, white noise creators, eye masks, ear plugs or fans – I am sure there are many more!

▶ Do not be afraid to try sleep medication and vitamins. Speak to your doctor about what may be best for you.

▶ Make sure that you are eating a healthy, balanced diet, as in 'M is for Medication'. Reduce the amount of caffeine or sugar that you consume throughout the day to encourage your brain to slow down towards the evening.

▶ Remember that you are not alone and there is nothing wrong with you for not being able to sleep. It is perfectly natural that we would want to stay awake if our minds are not ready to turn off, but we will try to help ourselves switch them off because we know it is going to be better for us in the long run. Be kind to yourself.

▶ At the same time, be strict with your thoughts. If you find yourself lying awake, ruminating on something that you don't need to be thinking about, firmly tell yourself that 'now is not the time to be thinking about this' and choose to focus on something else.

▸ Think about speaking to your workplace, as in 'J is for Jobs', about flexible working hours if you find that you have more energy at a certain time of day.

▸ See 'P is for Procrastination' on tips for how to get up in the morning – the secret is just forcing yourself to do it, nothing more! Count to five and make yourself uncomfortable for a second, hop out of bed and face the day. I have a 'getting out of bed' playlist that helps motivate me!

is for Time Management

Did you know?

- Research has proven that people with ADHD have difficulties in being able to assess time and feel as though time is passing them by without being able to complete tasks accurately and well. These skills are said to be critical for effective time management (Ptacek *et al.*, 2019).

- People with ADHD tend to be very heavily influenced by their external surroundings and can struggle with future-planning. We can have a sense of time that is 'now' or 'not now' (Ptacek *et al.*, 2019).

- Medical treatment of ADHD has been found to normalise time perception.

ADHD is very strongly linked with problems relating to time management. This is because we tend to only have two senses of time: now and not now. This chapter is focused on building in a pause between our thoughts and actions, because for people with ADHD, there is no pause. The make-up of our brains mean that we respond automatically, seemingly without thinking, or at least very quickly.

Dr Barkley explains the impact of ADHD on our brains' ability to manage time very well (Barkley, 2017):

1. **Hindsight:** When faced with a decision, ADHD-ers cannot visualise the relevant past in their mind's eye. We don't have the theatre in our minds that allow us to replay our previous experiences as others do.

2. **Foresight:** As a result of being unable to look back, we are unable to anticipate the future. We can't look back and plan for the future, because we have no context within which to come up with these thoughts.

3. **Mental voice:** ADHD also impacts the brain in such in a way that we cannot hear our 'mind's voice', the self-parenting voice that tells us to make 'sensible' choices instead of what we automatically want to do. This is why we struggle following instructions or rules – the voices that are supposed to regulate us don't show up in our brains.

4. **Mind's heart:** Our emotions are our motivations, and if we cannot manage our emotions, then we cannot manage our motivations either. Our emotions are the fuel tank for all future-directed behaviour, and so this is why ADHD-ers cannot motivate themselves like those without it can. Our motivation of how long and hard we can work will always be dependent on our environment and its immediate consequences. If there are no consequences for us, then we cannot focus.

   Dr Barkley compares homework, as in the completion of a maths problem on paper, with playing video games. The latter provides a constant source of external stimulation and consequences, whereas in doing our homework, we would have to wait until the next day to feel any external consequences. Maybe this is why I often did mine on the way to school!

5. **Mind's playground:** This is our ability to plan and problem solve. Due to the above impairments, ADHD-ers struggle to think of multiple possible future options or solutions at the same time, which is a necessary part of problem solving.

Dr Barkley says we should try to minimise the time between events happening, the responses that we prepare and the outcomes of what we are doing.

The concept of waiting between having a thought and acting on it is what underpins many ADHD symptoms, such as impulsivity. It is literally not being able to think things through properly. We are directed by reason, consequences and immediate external stimulus.

Having ADHD means that we have to train our brains in *patience.* It can feel hard not to want to do everything at once, or not at all, but this ultimately requires us to trust ourselves to able to manage our time and energy appropriately so that we don't burn ourselves out. We don't always need to reply to every email or request immediately. We can wait, think about it, and return to it when we are ready.

There are different kinds of decisions, from more subconscious ones about what to eat for breakfast to deciding what to spend money on, or a big life decision about ending a relationship, for example.

If you're feeling either very rushed into making a decision or paralysed by all of the different overwhelming options, it can be helpful to consider things from the below angles. The more we consciously think things through from all different points, the more these will become automatically ingrained into our brains!

→ **Our past:** Try to remember any similar situations that you have encountered previously, how you felt about them and any lessons learned. For example, saying yes to something you didn't really want to do, letting somebody down and feeling guilty as a result.

→ **Our future:** What will this situation look like in one week, one month or one year? Do we have any pre-existing commitments that could cause a conflict with this decision? Would we still want to be doing this in a year, for example?

→ **What the decision will involve in reality:** This means the boring bits. For example, if we are considering a new job, have we thought through all of the potentially negative aspects, as well as the positive? Have we thought about what our daily life will look like, our commute, colleagues, workload? Do we have any notice periods to work through?

→ **Other people:** How might our decision impact others? For example, if we are considering moving to a new country, how would this impact our partner or family?

→ **Potential negative consequences:** This requires weighing up the good against the bad. For example, if we are lending money to someone, what will we do if they are unable to return it? Is there any way we can take practical steps to plan for such a situation? How long-lasting would the positive consequences be?

→ **Opportunity cost:** What will this decision cost us? What could we use the time, energy or money for if we were not doing this? For example, if we were planning to spend £20 on takeout from a restaurant, what else could we use that £20 for?

→ **How long we have to make the decision:** Do we have to do it *right now*? (Hint: usually the answer will be no!). If you can take your time in deciding, take it. Things often look different the next day.

→ **Whether we actually want to do it:** This may involve checking in with ourselves and spotting any tension in our bodies. Does the thought of saying yes make you clench your jaw, for example? How do you *feel* about it?

How to manage your time

→ **Make a time management plan by using a calendar.** The plan accounts for your time overall, how much time is spent at work and at home. By separating out your time into manageable, scheduled chunks in advance, you can set yourself key focuses for these areas, such as 'work on X' or 'relax'. It is good to have a copy to hand on your phone, computer or printed out on your wall.

→ **Dedicate some time each morning to planning your day and deciding what to prioritise, setting a 'to-do' list.** Try to limit it to three manageable tasks per day, with the ones you don't want to do first. As ADHD-ers are externally motivated, it may be helpful to write this on a whiteboard and set yourself reminders such as scheduled alerts or post-it notes.

→ **Separate any general tasks into 'important but not urgent', 'important and urgent', 'urgent but not important', and 'not urgent and not important' lists.** Prioritise those which are urgent and important and resolve to tackle the rest tomorrow. Write any distracting thoughts that pop up which are not urgent or important down on your list – it really helps to have them down on paper and out of your head!

→ **Spend a few days recording how long it takes you to complete different tasks** to gain a realistic understanding of time and how long certain tasks take you to complete.

→ **Always remember to give yourself more time than you think you will need** and to allocate time for breaks.

→ **Dedicate a certain amount of time each day to checking your emails, setting an automatic reply for other times.** It is also very helpful to block in 'desk time' to your work calendar, so that you will not be disturbed or distracted.

→ **When planning time in relation to a specific project or deadline, set yourself a series of deadlines that will help you stay motivated.** For example, these could be to finish a first draft on a certain date. It can be very helpful to have an 'accountability buddy' to do this with!

→ **When focusing on a project, concentrate on how to break this down into different sections and then break the sections down into individual tasks.** Remember to appropriate each task to the relevant person – it is unlikely that you will have sole responsibility for a certain project without anyone else. Work with these people, setting realistic check-in points for both of you – such as weekly phone calls – and don't be afraid to ask for help if you aren't sure.

is for Unite

Did you know?

- The first All Party Parliamentary Group for ADHD launched in the Houses of Parliament in January 2018. At the time of writing, meetings are ongoing, with the aim of raising awareness about ADHD, bringing positive changes to the lives of people living with ADHD and to connect Parliament with organisations and charities involved in ADHD.

- There have been very successful campaigns such as the Umbrella Project, raising awareness about neurodiversity, such as the fact that one in five people are neurodivergent (ADHD Foundation, n.d.).

- There are ADHD-focused communities and support groups available globally,[1] where you can connect with other people who are having similar experiences to you. You are not alone.

Having ADHD can be extremely lonely and isolating. Strong interpersonal relationships can be very difficult to establish and maintain, due to the symptoms of ADHD, such as emotional dysregulation and hyper-sensitivity to potential rejection.

These symptoms can be very lonely to experience, and it may be a revelation to even read a book such as this to see that you are not alone in how you are feeling. I was taken to a

---

1   I recommend ADHD Unlocked: https://members.adhdunlocked.co.uk/ ~access/a1c91f.

mental health meeting[2] in Australia by a friend and felt so relieved to see that other seemingly 'normal' people were having similar experiences to me. This can be particularly important if talking about mental health isn't something you are used to, or if the people in your life have negative views towards it or ADHD in particular.

The reality is that millions of people throughout the world have ADHD and feel exactly the same way as you do. Around 1.5 million adults in the UK are estimated to have ADHD (BBC News, 2018), but only 120,000 are formally diagnosed. It can take up to seven years to be diagnosed in some parts of the UK, and this situation is similar worldwide. Around 6.4 million adults in America are said to have ADHD, but they do not enjoy access to free or subsidised healthcare as we do in the UK (Holland & Riley, 2014).

Long waiting times and financial constraints may mean that you are unable to be diagnosed with ADHD when you need to be or access a therapist to talk to. This can feel like your life is on hold, especially if you think it is likely that you may have ADHD and want to take medication for it. I hope that this book has shown there are different ways of managing ADHD without the requirement for an official medical diagnosis.

Having a community that you can talk to about ADHD and your experiences without fearing that they will judge you is truly life-changing. There are a variety of different ways that you could do this.

---

2   https://www.onewaveisallittakes.com

Unite with other people who have ADHD

There are communities of ADHD-ers all over the world. The brilliant thing about the internet is that it is easier than ever to find and communicate with people who share similar interests to you.

It can be very rewarding to speak online to other people who have ADHD, although it is important to make sure that you are safe and follow usual internet safety procedures, such as not giving away personal information or meeting people from the internet whom you do not trust 100 per cent – especially alone! Avoid meeting anyone from the internet in a private location and try to always take somebody else with you if you do plan to meet up.

As someone who is open about having ADHD on the internet, this could make you a target for people who want to manipulate you, who can use ADHD as a commonality between you. They may understand how to play on your emotions and groom you into sharing much more information than you feel comfortable with, so please be careful.

This being said, online ADHD communities can be incredibly helpful and a great source of community for someone with ADHD. There are thousands of people available to support each other and provide validation of feelings and experiences associated with ADHD, and often very helpful advice is offered in these communities. It is important to recognise how much dependence you may develop on these communities, and to remember that ultimately the internet is not the real world, but to use it as a resource.

Some communities I would recommend joining are:

→ www.adhdunlocked.co.uk

→ www.facebook.com/groups/additudemag

→ www.reddit.com/r/ADHD

→ https://chadd.org

→ https://aadduk.org

→ www.iampayingattention.co.uk

→ www.kaleidoscopesociety.com

You may also have an ADHD support group in your local area. Check online[3] to see what already exists or consider setting up your own!

Unite with organisations

If you are interested in connecting with people who understand ADHD and potentially even volunteering to help others, it could be worth looking into the organisations that are providing resources for ADHD-ers. Some of these are below:

→ **ADHD Foundation:** 'The Neurodiversity Charity' focuses on raising awareness about the neurodiversity associated with ADHD, such as with the 'Umbrella Project 2019' which led to installations around the UK celebrating the 'superpowers' that ADHD can bring. They also have an annual conference and training courses available for professionals working with ADHD, amongst other resources.

---

3   www.meetup.com

→ **ADDISS:** 'The National Attention Deficit Disorder Information and Support Service' provides people-friendly information and resources about ADHD to anyone who needs assistance, including hosting support groups and conferences about ADHD.

→ **ADHD UK:** This is a charity created by people with ADHD for people with ADHD. They host weekly support sessions, self-screening tools, helpful information about diagnosis and drop in advice clinics.

→ **ADHD Action:** This organisation focuses on campaigning to raise awareness about ADHD and has an impressive campaign for the UK government to create an ADHD Act which would provide additional resources and strategies for ADHD-ers.

→ **AADD-UK:** This charity focuses on raising awareness of ADHD in adulthood, providing a considerable wealth of information and resources on their website.

→ **ADHD Girls:** This organisation has a dual mission to empower girls and women with ADHD to thrive in society and improve societal understanding of ADHD through digital campaigns, talks and events within education and work settings.

You could also start your own!

Unite: Other resources

There is a wealth of information online about ADHD and great books available to learn more about whichever area you are most interested in (in addition to this one)!

ADDitude magazine is a very valuable resource that has existed since 1998. The website is extremely comprehensive, with articles, newsletters, webinars, symptom tests and an online community.

Some excellent books that have helped me include:

→ *ADHD 2.0* by Edward M. Hallowell, MD, and John J. Ratey, MD

→ *Driven to Distraction* by Edward M. Hallowell, MD, and John J. Ratey, MD

→ *The Teenage Girl's Guide to Living Well with ADHD* by Sonia Ali

→ *You Mean I'm Not Lazy, Stupid or Crazy?* by Kate Kelly and Peggy Ramundo

→ *Scattered Minds: The Origin and Healing of Attention Deficit Disorder* by Dr Gabor Mate

→ *The ADHD Effect on Marriage: Understand and Rebuild Your Relationship in Six Steps* by Melissa Orlov

→ *Chained to the Desk: A Guidebook for Workaholics, Their Partners and Children, and the Clinicians Who Treat Them* by Bryan E. Robinson, PhD

→ *Refuse to Choose* by Barbara Sher

→ *Crucial Conversations: Tools for Talking When Stakes Are High* by Kerry Patterson *et al.*

→ *The Organized Mind: Thinking Straight in the Age of Information Overload* by Daniel Levitin

is for Vices

Did you know?

- ADHD has been strongly linked to problems with substance abuse, such as alcohol and drug addiction. This may be because of the tendency to be impulsive, difficulties with planning ahead, and as a way of self-medicating.

- It's estimated that about 25 per cent of adults being treated for alcohol and substance abuse have ADHD (Watson, 2020).

- Adults with ADHD have a higher mortality rate than those without and are nine times more likely to end up in prison than those of a similar age and background who do not have ADHD (Born to Be ADHD, 2017).

ADHD-ers may find that they have some bad habits because of our ADHD symptoms, such as impulsivity and low self-esteem. These vices tend to be 'quick fixes' of dopamine, easily accessible but with potentially life-destroying side-effects. There may be a range of reasons why ADHD-ers are susceptible to these, such as the addictive nature of the activity itself, as in the case of drugs, or as a way of self-medicating, such as drinking alcohol to stop 'thinking.'

Such behaviour is devastating because it tends to not only be dangerous but also worsen ADHD symptoms in the long run. It perpetuates a cycle of impulsivity, self-sabotage and failure, leading to more bad decisions.

We may also find ourselves seeking adrenaline or excessive stimulation to manage symptoms, such as a restless mind. This can result in making reckless decisions and taking dangerous risks, such as speeding and committing crimes. Research has found that people with ADHD are twice as likely to commit a crime as those without it (LancUK, 2012). This perpetuates the negative cycle of low self-esteem and can become addictive behaviour in the chase for the 'high'. The vices associated with ADHD can also be very expensive and lead to an inability to save money or getting into debt, as in 'F is for Finance'.

Alcohol and drugs may be particularly attractive options to someone with ADHD because of the way that they 'turn off' thoughts and appear to calm us down. Addictions of these kind tend to destroy not only our own lives but also those of the people who care about us.

Alternatively, our vices could be a little more 'socially acceptable' in the form of caffeine or sugar. These are problematic as they can go unseen by others and be written off as 'normal' behaviour. I used to quite literally live on chocolate bars and drink ten coffees a day, thinking that it had no effect on me. In reality, this kept me in a cycle of highs and lows, of being able to focus for short periods and then not being able to focus at all.

Many people I know with ADHD have similarly sugar-fuelled diets and chaotic energy spikes, which can be terrible for someone with ADHD, who is likely to already be on an energy rollercoaster. This isn't even to mention the negative impacts such habits can have on our general health.

Another category of vices could be general distractions.

These could include smoking (as something to do with your hands or to 'calm' you down), video games, social media, binge-watching television, online shopping – anything that seems like relaxation but is actually a form of numbing yourself. These activities normally don't result in feeling positive afterwards, but often leave you feeling worse than you did when you entered the vortex.

The excitement that ADHD-ers may feel when they are 'hyper- focused' and doing something they enjoy can result in addictive behaviour in the form of burning themselves out. This addictive behaviour can be all-consuming and quite literally take over your life to the exclusion of everything else, which is, generally speaking, not a healthy pattern of focus for your brain to have. I often feel like my brain is either turned 'on' or 'off', with no in-between – like a light switch. This behaviour in itself is negative because it can lead to exhaustion, as in 'B is for Burnout', and result in other negative side-effects such as not eating or looking after yourself properly.

The key is finding moderation and balance. This is very difficult for me – for example, I tend to be either completely vegan or a meat eater, with nothing in the middle. This comes back to setting ourselves too high expectations which we are never able to meet.

We are human beings and it is completely normal and acceptable to live however we want to live. There is no right or wrong rulebook for us to follow, but there is our own intuition about what makes us feel happy and healthy, and what makes us feel unhappy and unhealthy.

Following on from this, there are no 'set' vices other than

those criminalised by law, but we can use our own common sense to understand what this means for us. There are all types of addictions and things that we use to avoid our feelings, from shopping to work, alcohol to coffee, and so on.

I would really recommend speaking to a qualified professional such as a therapist or doctor if you are struggling with dangerous habits, such as alcohol, gambling or drug addictions. They will be able to give you the help you need.

In some milder cases, ADHD coaches may be able to support you with changing negative habits by enabling you to set up new routines and structures, as in 'E is for Executive Functioning'.

Sometimes these issues may come to light in coaching when we examine what's stopping a person from doing what they want to do, such as going out clubbing, or staying up late on social media. I've seen clients overcome issues relating to alcohol, smoking, binge-eating and social media use, but they have to *want* to do these things for themselves. You are ultimately the only person who can decide how to live your life – how do you want to spend it?

Identifying bad habits

1. Make an honest assessment of your life. Write down all the bad habits that you may have had in the past, up until any that you may have today. These could include, for example: smoking, alcohol, caffeine, sugar, reckless driving, phone addiction, social media, video games, over-exercising, online shopping.

2. Assess each habit and how it is impacting your life. Write

down all of the negative side-effects of the habit (past or present) and how much time you generally dedicate to it.

3. Now identify your 'top three' habits from this list and pick one that you would like to stop.

Replacing bad habits

To stop your bad habit, moderation is key. You can create a new habit to replace it by doing something consistently every day for 28 days. As everybody is motivated differently, to stop a bad habit you need to understand yourself and make your own tailored plan that you can stick to.

I would generally advise against trying to stop something cold turkey, as this can easily set you up for failure. Trusting yourself to slowly change your behaviour over time is important when it comes to choosing how to live on a long-term basis.

1. Write down any ways that you have stopped doing negative things in the past, such as going to 12-step programmes.

2. Identify what you are motivated by. Why do you want to stop the bad habits? Make a plan for how you can motivate yourself to want to change your behaviour.

3. Break down how you can stop the bad habit into small manageable chunks. You may find that this works best by setting yourself one goal per week, or a tiny task per day. Try to think about how you can slowly reduce the effect of the habit – for example, if you smoke, cut down on one cigarette per day for a month.

4. Ask for help. This is especially important if the habit is something that is particularly addictive or dangerous, and, as above, it is advisable to speak to a qualified professional instead of trying to tackle it by yourself. Generally speaking, the people in our life should want us to be happy, and willing to help support us with changing our behaviour if we ask them. Speak to somebody that you trust and tell them about what you are doing, asking them for their help. This could involve checking in on your progress, or simply being available for a conversation when you need them, for example.

5. Identify any potential triggers or blocks to your success and prepare in advance for them. For example, this could be going out with friends which makes you want to drink alcohol or smoke. Avoid the triggers completely or as much as you can, planning for any unavoidable situations. It might be helpful to explain to people such as your friends what you are trying to do; they might suggest doing a different activity to help support you.

6. Plan to replace the vice with a positive habit. You will likely be receiving additional time and money as a result of giving up your vice so use this to be kind to yourself, such as spending the money saved each month on a yoga membership.

Remember not to beat yourself up if you do not stick to your plan. Changing your behaviour takes a tremendous amount of willpower and focus, which ADHD-ers tend to not have by the bucketload! Be kind to yourself throughout the process and simply get back on the horse if you fall off, learning from the reasons why.

It's important to remember that substances such as alcohol and drugs can be extremely dangerous and highly addictive for everybody, let alone those with ADHD. Sometimes we may not be able to overcome these issues, and it's important to be able to understand the difference between problematic habits and serious addictions.

Some resources for addictions are listed below, but I'd recommend speaking to your doctor as soon as possible to get the support you need.

→ UK Narcotics Anonymous: www.ukna.org

→ Gamblers Anonymous: www.gamblersanonymous.org.uk

→ Alcoholics Anonymous: www.alcoholics-anonymous.org.uk

→ Workaholics Anonymous: workaholics-anonymous.org

→ Step Change Debt Charity: www.stepchange.org

→ UK National Debtline: www.nationaldebtline.org

→ Be Gamble Aware: www.begambleaware.org

→ Drug Wise: www.drugwise.org.uk

→ Mind: www.mind.org.uk

→ Beating Addictions: www.beatingaddictions.co.uk

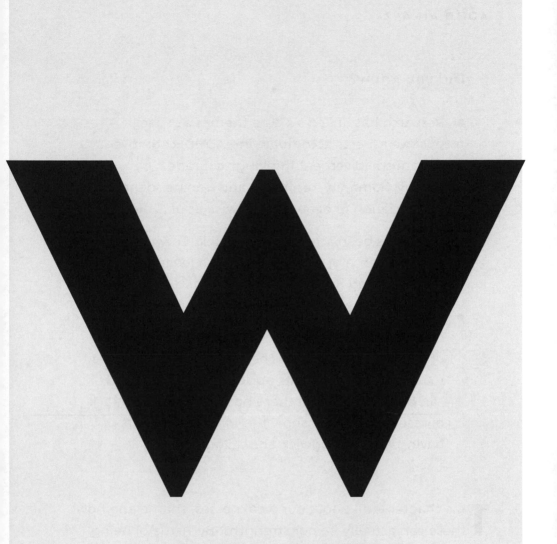

is for Weaknesses

Did you know?

- Research has linked six core themes as specific positive aspects accompanying ADHD: cognitive dynamism (divergent thinking), courage, energy, humanity, resilience and transcendence (appreciation of beauty) (Sedgwick *et al.*, 2018).

- ADHD has been scientifically associated with having a strong sense of integrity and with feelings of being authentic and honest (Sedgwick *et al.*, 2018).

- A 2018 study found that hardly any empirical research had been done about the positive aspects of ADHD previously. Searches for this kind of content mainly produced results about treatment – which can be beneficial, but there has been a distinct lack of research done to show the inherent benefits of having ADHD (Sedgwick *et al.*, 2018).

This chapter is all about our weaknesses, shame and how these can actually be our strengths. By virtue of being called a 'disorder', ADHD can make us feel that there is something wrong with us – that we are somehow weaker than others. It can be easy to ruminate on this and to see ourselves as fundamentally flawed, but what is really important to remember is that your brain is just wired differently.

There are literal differences in your brain to others, which cause your ADHD symptoms. This isn't a bad thing, it's just different – which is actually a *good* thing. Matt Haig, Zooey

Deschanel and Solange Knowles have ADHD – to name but a few leading minds in our world. If we all thought exactly the same way, there would never be any new, original or creative things happening – the world would be much greyer.

Here are some of the weaknesses that we might feel we have as ADHD-ers, and how they can be turned into strengths:

Procrastinating and unable to finish tasks = authenticity, creativity and learning to use our hyper-focus superpower!

Procrastinating can be frustrating when we *really* need to get something done, objectively speaking, and literally cannot. For example, finishing a big project for work or school. We might have beaten ourselves up throughout our lives for not being able to concentrate, missing deadlines or not doing as a good a job as we would have liked to do.

The secret here is that you are trying to fit into a box, and you aren't meant to fit into a box. It can really help to remember that these tasks we set ourselves are ultimately small parts of our lives, and each experience helps teach us something new.

Having ADHD means that unless you actually want to do something, it will be more difficult than it would be for a neurotypical person, but the payoff is that when you find something you *do* really want to do, you can do it at a superpower level. Hyper-focus is often associated with creativity and being super-productive, and research has found that adults with ADHD had more real-time creative achievements than those without (White & Shah, 2006).

We can learn how to become organised, and how to beat

procrastination. However, we don't have to give up our authenticity to do this – we can learn how to use our motivation to be super-productive at anything we put our minds to!

Impulsivity and changing our minds a lot = living an exciting, fun and courageous life!

The tendency to not think things through before we do them can make ADHD-ers 'yes' people. Whilst it is definitely worth learning how to control this impulsivity muscle (see 'N is for No'), seeing as there is only so much one person is capable of, it can also mean that we are very brave.

We might find ourselves in a range of exciting situations, as a result of seeking stimulation, from skydiving to writing a book, learning about our latest interest or trying out a new career. ADHD-ers tend to live memorable, full lives! Life is ultimately for living, and having a fearless, spontaneous nature can mean that we don't hold ourselves back. It's good for us to learn how to spot when it *is* a good idea to hold ourselves back, as in 'V is for Vices', but there is nothing wrong with being an interested person. Curiosity has been strongly linked to ADHD, along with being open to experiences and having a desire to learn (Zuss, 2012).

Changing our minds can result in a lot of shame, and problems in our relationships, as in 'L is for Love'. We might feel like we aren't able to stick at anything and feel a lot of guilt for quitting things we have committed to. However, nothing lasts forever anyway. People have a few different careers throughout their lives. In 2019, 42 per cent of marriages ended in divorce in England and Wales

(Office of National Statistics, 2o2o). Sixty per cent of new businesses fail in the first three years (*May*, 2o19). We can fool ourselves into thinking we need to pick one job, relationship, house and so on for our entire lives, and that to do anything else is failure.

It's not – it's being human. Whilst it is very good to learn how to control our initial decisions about what we want to do (and how much energy or time we can put into that), there is nothing wrong with trying things out and failing. Every failure teaches us something new, and we tend to be good at bouncing back, which is the secret to success!

Emotional dysregulation = extremely empathetic, energetic and likeable people!

The differences in how ADHD-ers relate to others can sometimes cause problems, as we've seen in 'L is for Love' and 'X is for X-treme Differences in Women'. However, it can also result in beautiful, deep connections and incredibly empathetic people. Having ADHD can be exceptionally lonely at times, because we suffer with a lot of shame for being 'different' to others; this may have originated in childhood, when we were all supposed to fit in and achieve the same mandated level of success in our exams.

Being different can be hard, but it can also be great. I can usually tell when I meet another person who has ADHD, because they are immediately extremely warm, funny, creative and deep. They are truly interested in our conversation, instead of making small talk. They have interesting lives and are fun to talk to, even if our conversations can be a chain of us interrupting each other out of excitement!

Suffering from rejection throughout our life because of being different can mean that we do feel extreme pain when we sense it happening again as adults, but this also means we are capable of extreme love. We can feel things on a broad spectrum of rainbow colours, and it makes for an interesting experience of being alive. As we have typically suffered a lot of pain in the past, we tend to be hyper-sensitive to others' pain and tend to not be afraid to stand up for others when we see unfairness happening.

I believe that the majority of ADHD-ers are exceptionally kind, sensitive and compassionate. Being driven by the happiness of others is not always good if it's ignoring ourselves, as in 'N is for No', but, as a general principle, caring about other people is something to be celebrated. ADHD has been scientifically linked to optimism, persuasiveness and an energy that vitalises and inspires others around them (Sedgwick *et al.*, 2018) – great qualities to have in an employee, for example!

Although we might struggle with maintaining drama-free relationships, I like to think that we will ultimately attract people who are willing to work through any problems with us just as we would with them, because it's worth it. *You* are worth it.

Struggling with tasks that require sustained attention = creative, out-of-the-box and clever thinker!

As in 'E is for Executive Functioning', we can learn how to train our attention and motivate ourselves into doing tasks that we might struggle with, such as organising bills, even if it doesn't come naturally to us.

If a person has undiagnosed ADHD and simply cannot do these tasks, they might be beating themselves up and too embarrassed to tell anybody about it. Understanding that our brains are simply neurologically different when it comes to our ability to do this kind of work makes it much easier to be compassionate with ourselves and ask for help, because it is not our fault.

This neurological 'deficiency' is often compensated by thinking creatively. ADHD-ers may be able to connect dots that a neurotypical person wouldn't think to put together, have innovative ideas and think in amazingly original ways. Richard Branson dropped out of school when he was 15, starting his own magazine and going on to become a billionaire. You are not stupid – the system we have for measuring intelligence is. Exams and schoolwork are not the only ways of being clever. Learning how to do arithmetic and chemistry equations are unlikely to help you figure out how to get a job or do your taxes.

Learn to recognise your own intelligence and watch it grow, as in 'C is for Confidence'.

Overthinking and being over-energised = having a lot of excess energy to use up!

Although it's pretty universally accepted that we need sleep, there's no reason why you shouldn't use your energy up when it is most effective. For example, if you work better later at night rather than in the mornings, who's to say you should be working in the mornings? When we know how to put boundaries in place to ensure we are meeting our own needs, as in 'Y is for Your Body', we can then work around that scaffolding to live our most brilliant lives.

Having a lot of energy means that we can do lots of things and make the most of our lives. Whilst it's important that we relax and direct our energy into the *right* things for us, such as exercise or projects that we enjoy, it is a great thing that we have so much energy, and once we learn how to manage it most effectively, it becomes extremely valuable.

Part of understanding our ADHD is being able to manage this energy and be in control of it, so that it's sustainable. However, we shouldn't be trying to make ourselves small, feel shame about ourselves or live a life that is not within our full potential – having this much energy is an amazing thing, and inspires others around us.

Being sensitive to rejection and having low self-esteem = an incredibly resilient, resourceful and strong survivor!

All lives are fraught with rejection, which, if you have ADHD, can be especially difficult. Growing up with a neurodivergent brain means that you think differently to 'most' people, and simply surviving in a world that isn't designed for you is quite an achievement! Researchers have found that ADHD-ers cope well with stress, which makes us resilient – we have been able to survive despite adverse conditions (Sedgwick *et al.*, 2018). This may be why we are excellent in a crisis, or under pressure – we are used to it!

Ironically, the impulsivity and low self-esteem that can accompany ADHD can mean we put ourselves in positions where we may be likely to fail or encounter rejection (which might be why we are always on the lookout for it!). This has definitely been the case for me, where I have had zero expectations of doing things, such as publishing this book, just the hope that it might help somebody who needs it. Releasing ourselves from expectations, judgement from others and 'looking weird' (I gave up on that a long time ago!) frees us to chase our interests with a unique sense of resilience.

Although I can be sensitive to rejection from the people close to me, being bullied throughout childhood and rejected to my face more times than I can possibly count as a fashion model mean that I am pretty good at brushing off the general judgements of others. I think a lot of ADHD-ers have a similar sense of resilience in not being afraid to fail, because we are so used to failing that anything else is simply a nice surprise!

If you have ADHD, please remember that you are the furthest thing from weak. ADHD doesn't define you as a person, but it does mean that you are exceptionally strong for living in a world that doesn't cater for your neurodiversity. We are survivors, and living with ADHD can be incredibly difficult, especially if we don't know that we even have it. Once we understand what it is, we can then develop it to unlock the potential inside of us.

is for X-treme Differences in Women

Did you know?

- One in four women with ADHD (23.5%) has attempted suicide, compared to 3.3 per cent of women without ADHD (Fuller-Thompson *et al.*, 2020).

- Boys are five times more likely to be diagnosed with ADHD than girls, although in later life, case numbers are roughly similar for men and women. This means women and girls are experiencing ADHD misdiagnosis due to misconceptions around symptoms (Ratcliffe, 2022).

- ADHD is strongly impacted by hormonal fluctuations such as oestrogen, which means symptoms can change significantly in relation to menstruation, perimenopause or menopause, for example (CHADD, 2017).

Throughout my life, I was called stupid, lazy, dramatic and an attention seeker, which is what I believed about myself by the time I was diagnosed with ADHD at 25 years old. This makes me incredibly sad for the younger version of myself who missed out on understanding herself and living her life, instead of obsessively believing that she was somehow broken. I missed out on the happiness, self-acceptance and joy of living I've had since then.

Despite me seeing doctors in childhood for being excessively clumsy or unable to listen, as in 'Y is for Your Body', ADHD was never mentioned as a possibility. As in 'D is for Diagnosis', when I sought medical help as an adult for the severe nature of my symptoms, I was told that I might just have 'emotional issues'.

I strongly believe that the stigma relating to girls and women being 'emotional' is resulting in hundreds of thousands of us who need help being denied it, even when we make the brave step of asking for it. At the time of writing, the ADHD diagnosis criteria in the NICE guidelines (NICE, 2018) do not include emotional symptoms, despite immense research proving their importance.

As a coach, I now work with countless strong, resilient, intelligent, passionate, inspirational and creative women who have to fight every day to be heard, and to exist as themselves in a world where it's more 'convenient' for them to be someone else. They've all been gaslit, shamed, ignored and made to feel as though they were simply being 'too much', like they're simply not trying hard enough to be 'normal'.

My experience

When I first learned about ADHD, I thought it could only affect hyperactive boys in class. Far from being loud and disruptive in class, I was often literally falling asleep and staring out of the window!

I skipped P.E. every week but could spend an entire day sitting on my laptop, so I didn't see myself as hyperactive at all. However, I knew that I'd always definitely been *mentally* hyperactive, and that since childhood, I'd been trying to figure out how to shut my brain up, which I eventually found in binge-drinking alcohol. I can easily go a month without exercising, but my brain can't go a minute without exploding with thoughts.

I'd also managed to get good exam results and graduate from university. Despite knowing I definitely struggled to pay attention in class, I'd somehow managed to teach myself entire subjects a week before the exams, to the point that my schoolteacher asked the entire class if I'd cheated because of my results!

This is what having undiagnosed ADHD as a girl can feel like – as though you're cheating and lying, just by being yourself. I felt like my strong mood swings were just me being 'crazy', and as though I was constantly masking my inner chaos. Whenever doctors told me I was fine, I'd thank them and leave smiling, feeling the inner dread of knowing I was definitely not fine.

I'd go to therapy sessions and speak non-stop for an hour, cementing myself into another week of ruminating on my past. It felt like somebody else had the remote control to my brain, and I couldn't trust myself. I kept moving around the world to solve my problems, with no stable job, place to live, or support network of friends or family.

By the time I was diagnosed, I was extremely suicidal, having struggled in the darkness by myself for so many years. I struggled to even accept this diagnosis, researching the symptoms and not resonating fully with them, which is part of why I wrote this book!

Why ADHD is missed in females

I believe the reason that girls and women find it so difficult to get diagnosed with ADHD includes the below factors:

Symptoms presentation

As emotional symptoms aren't even included in the diagnostic criteria for ADHD, it's unsurprising that those we may experience in relation to our emotions might be misdiagnosed or ignored. I strongly believe that if a person with ADHD isn't physically hyperactive, they are mentally hyperactive – all my clients have been proof of this!

This can feel like all the hyperactivity of what we imagine as a child running around a classroom is internalised inside our brains. ADHD symptoms such as overthinking, wildly strong mood swings, indecisiveness and Rejection Sensitive Dysphoria may be written off as generalised anxiety or 'emotional issues', as happened to me.

As women tend to internalise symptoms much more than men, with symptoms such as inattentiveness and disorganisation, they can easily be missed due to not being as obviously 'disruptive' to other people.

Medical professionals may be more likely to associate these symptoms with other conditions for women, especially if they're not presenting with physical hyperactivity that can be seen externally.

The strong correlation of emotional symptoms to females with ADHD may be as a result of our hormonal fluctuations. As our symptoms change throughout the month in accordance with our menstrual cycle – we might find we experience extremely bad PMS, for example – we might think these are purely hormonal fluctuations, rather being connected to ADHD. Many women with ADHD may only learn about this during their perimenopause or menopause, due to the hormonal changes in their bodies.

Masking and coping strategies

As in 'N is for No', people with ADHD have a tendency to people-please, which is especially prevalent in females. We live in a society where we have impossibly huge pressures and expectations on us in terms of how we look and behave, and what we achieve. This is exacerbated by social media, which gives us all a platform to display the highlights of our lives, possibly leading us to compare our real selves to filtered highlights of our past!

As a result, females with ADHD may learn early on how to mask their symptoms, as I did. This makes the mental hyperactivity and anxiety in my brain worse as I have to layer every situation in my life with thoughts about how to appear 'normal'. I'm constantly questioning myself, and literally copied other girls in my class as a child to figure out how to best fit in.

I also grew up believing it was normal to need to make multiple to-do lists and have to write down my thoughts constantly to keep track of them. Women may develop better coping strategies and overcompensate by putting in an unsustainable amount of effort, as in 'B is for Burnout', which may only become obvious later on, such as after a significant life change.

The difficulty with this is that we might be masking in areas of our life to such extreme degrees that we may not even realise it ourselves. This can be especially true given impairments in our self-awareness, as in 'E is for Executive Functioning'. We might find it very difficult to insist on help as a result, such as me agreeing with the doctor who said I was fine, and not understanding why!

Co-existing conditions

As in 'A is for ADHD', there is an extremely strong crossover with Autism, depression, anxiety, eating disorders, obesity, alcoholism, drug addiction, self-harm, and/or pre-menstrual syndrome. It's highly likely that ADHD exists with another condition alongside it, sometimes referred to as a co-morbidity.

As doctors such as GPs know more about conditions such as anxiety, they are easier to diagnose and prescribe medication for, whilst expert psychiatrists, who are more likely to spot ADHD, have years-long waiting lists on the NHS. This can avoid treating the root cause of issues – for example, I've experienced a significant reduction in my lifelong anxiety since taking ADHD medication, whereas anxiety medication made it worse.

This will obviously be different for everybody, and you should follow your doctor's advice (especially if you have a co-morbidity – any help is better than none!), but it's advisable to explicitly ask for an ADHD assessment if you feel you need it. You are entitled to this support, and even if you've been given help in one area, that doesn't mean that you don't have ADHD. Unfortunately, medical misdiagnosis can lead us to question ourselves and our experiences, but we are the only ones who know what it's truly like to be us.

Situational variability

As women may have found ways of coping with their ADHD with structures in place such as school, their symptoms may only become obvious later on in life. This happened to me when I graduated from university and couldn't handle what I saw as the 'real world'.

There's unfortunately still so much stigma in our society in relation to ADHD and mental health, including outdated ideas – ADHD was only diagnosable in adults from 2oo8! Previously, it was thought that if a person didn't display the 'traditional' symptoms as a child, they couldn't have ADHD.

I found it very difficult to seek out help, and even after being so publicly open years later, I still sometimes hear that I don't 'look like I have ADHD'. This may be because of the intense coping strategies I developed when undiagnosed and because of how much my life has changed since then, such as publishing books and working in law. I might be able to write a book, but I still can't wash my clothes, cook meals or manage bills without a huge amount of effort and support!

If you've met one person with ADHD, you've met one person with ADHD – it shows up differently in everybody, including at different stages in their lives, and particularly between women and men.

Tips

- ▶ If you think you have ADHD, seek out support – and don't stop fighting until you get it!

- ▶ Reach out to other girls or women with ADHD to find a support group, as in 'U is for Unite'.

- ▶ Keep a journal of your symptoms and feelings, and refer back to it when you're feeling unsure.

It may also be helpful to track this alongside your menstrual cycle to better prepare for how you may feel at different times of the month.

▸ Try to exercise for at least half an hour every day – aerobic exercise is one of the most important things we can do to improve our brain functioning, and it also improves our self-confidence (The Chesapeake Center, n.d.). From dancing around your bedroom to trying out a novelty class such as aerial yoga, it can be incredibly helpful for us to get out of our heads and into our bodies.

▸ Speak to people in your life about your experiences and ask them for support. I sometimes think of my life as spinning 18 plates at the same time, and if I drop one, they'll all smash on the floor, which might resonate! You deserve help, and learning how to ask for and receive this help can be life-changing. You don't have to do it all!

is for Your Body

Did you know?

- There is a lot of crossover between ADHD and Sensory Processing Disorder, which can result in misdiagnosis. ADHD can have an impact on the way we experience the world through our senses, resulting in physical manifestations, such as feeling the need to be constantly moving, or feeling excessively hot or cold.

- Research has connected problems with 'motor control' with children who have ADHD, finding that almost 50 per cent had difficulty balancing and controlling motor function (Pera, 2015). As we don't tend to outgrow our symptoms, this can also apply to adults – making us clumsy!

- A study of adults with ADHD found that 43 per cent of women had sensory over- and/or under-responsivity, compared to 22 per cent of men, suggesting that women with ADHD are more prone to sensory issues (Brown & Dunn, 2002).

ADHD affects our entire bodies. It has been commonly linked with differences relating to how we perceive the world through our senses, with some crossover of symptoms with Sensory Processing Disorder (SPD). This disorder is not recognised as a diagnosis, but rather a description of behaviour, which is said to exist when sensory signals are not organised into 'appropriate' behavioural and physiological responses by our nervous system.

This means that we might experience the world differently to neurotypical people. I don't think there is any one 'normal' way of perceiving the world – for example, the fact that we don't all like the same foods – but it's helpful to be aware of this so that you can understand yourself, and maybe others, a little better. By understanding your own body and sensitivities, you can better understand your own needs at any one time, which is really important for ADHD-ers to know how to do. Once you can understand your needs, you can communicate them better, because if we don't understand that we are frustrated by something, we can't explain that to others and instead are prone to having emotional reactions.

These issues may also not be impacted by ADHD medication and in some circumstances could indicate the presence of other conditions, such as Autism. There are many different possible 'disorders' in relation to the senses, such as auditory processing disorder, but the key thing to bear in mind is that it is just how you are experiencing the world. There isn't any right or wrong way to experience it, and there is no one-size-fits-all approach – even for one person, as it can change so quickly depending on our stress levels and environment.

It would have been incredibly helpful to know about this when I was a child. My parents thought that I had problems with hearing, because I seemed unable to listen and was always walking into things such as tables. Ironically, I was given fish oil, which has been proven to help with ADHD symptoms, as in 'M is for Medication', but the ADHD was completely missed until I was 25 years old.

An understanding of how sensory issues can arise in people who have ADHD can help us to spot ADHD better – it doesn't manifest physically in just one form, such as being unable to sit still. Frustration at tolerating these sensory manifestations can slowly build up in us, using a lot of mental energy, until we 'snap' and emotionally react, possibly without even understanding where this came from. By being aware of this, we can spot any problems early on and do something to make our existence in the world a little easier!

There are typically three ways that we can feel sensations differently to neurotypical people. A sensory over-responsivity can result in feeling things more intensely and may provoke a quicker and more dramatic response in the body, such as gagging at certain smells. A sensory under-responsivity may arise more subtly and take a longer time to react, such as failing to notice the pain caused by walking into objects until you spot bruises on your body in the morning! The third is a sensory craving, where we may have a nearly insatiable craving for sensory experiences, such as wanting to feel intense sensations, such as a very tight hug!

This is by no means an exhaustive list, but possible issues that could arise and ideas of how to deal with them, in relation to each of our eight senses are below:

Touch (tactile system)

Effect	Solution
Over- or undersensitivity to touch such as clothing, labels or jewellery. This could result in feeling uncomfortable and removing jewellery, for example (and losing it!).	Removing labels from clothes, wearing loose clothing or materials which make you feel as comfortable as possible. Layering up when getting dressed, and having dedicated places to put things, such as a bowl for jewellery on your desk, to avoid losing them.
Over- or undersensitivity to feeling pain.	Taking precautions such as sitting in an office chair at a desk when working.

Craving intense sensations, such as tight hugs.	Weighted blanket, deep tissue massages, hugs.
Dislike of specific sensations, such as being touched by others or certain materials.	Maintaining strong boundaries, adapting your environment to suit (e.g., bedsheets).
Aversion to bodily sensations, such as showering.	Maintaining strong personal hygiene in a routine, figuring out what you like, such as having baths instead of showers.
Craving constant tactile sensations, such as tapping a table or scratching skin.	Having a 'touch toy', such as a stress ball, or adapting your environment to suit you in a healthy way. I heard of one woman using a sandbox under her desk for her feet during the day!
Difficulty with fine motor tasks, such as buttoning clothes or tying laces.	Asking for help with tasks that cause difficulty or adapting your environment to suit, such as Velcro shoes!
Tendency to be messy or not perceiving mess in the same way as others (e.g., not seeing dust or crumbs on a surface or dressing in an uncoordinated way).	Hiring a cleaner(!) or, if living with others, asking them to show you what they perceive to be clean, developing a routine for cleaning, taking extra care when dressing and dedicating extra time to this.
Hypersensitivity to temperature, such as being excessively hot or cold or seeking certain states. Could also be prone to 'Seasonal Affective Disorder'.	Using a hot water bottle or hand warmers, layering clothes when getting dressed in the morning or taking additional layers with you, using techniques such as holding a frozen lemon to cool down or drinking ice-water. Using lights or goggles designed to simulate sunlight.

Smell (olfactory system)

Effect	Solution
Over- or undersensitivity to smells, such as food, which might not bother other people. This could include being bothered by certain smells or failing to distinguish between smells.	Adapting your environment suitably and avoiding certain smells if possible (e.g., by going out for a walk during lunchtime in the office).
Craving certain smells, such as strong perfume.	Understanding these cravings and fulfilling them (e.g., using incense or air freshener).
Being oblivious to smells, such as not being able to smell strong body odour.	Maintaining a strong personal hygiene routine, showering daily.

Sound (auditory system)

Effect	Solution
Over- or undersensitivity to certain sounds and volumes, such as not being able to fall asleep due to a low-volume sound that others might not be able to hear, such as a clock ticking.	Noise-cancelling headphones, white noise machine, regular check-ups at the doctors, ear-plugs, removing distractions from the bedroom such as clocks or switching off electronics at night.
Difficulty tolerating distractions or sounds in the form of noise, such as people speaking around you when trying to work or outside construction.	Noise-cancelling headphones, asking to work in a quieter part of the room or time of day, explaining to others the difficulties that you experience in a polite way!
Difficulty listening to others and processing what is being said, such as having delays between hearing and understanding, appearing not to hear certain sounds, needing instructions repeating.	Making extra effort to concentrate on people when they talk, writing down notes.
Craving certain sounds, such as loud music or making a lot of noise – or craving silence!	Noise-cancelling headphones, 'silent' musical instruments such as electronic drum kits.

Taste (gustatory system)

Effect	Solution
Over- or undersensitivity to tastes, such as being a 'picky' eater and only liking certain types of food.	Ensuring that you have a balanced diet with enough fruit and vegetables, avoiding situations where you might have to eat food you don't like or checking restaurant menus before dinners out. Creating a routine and planning meals.
Only eating foods at a certain temperature.	Adapting your environment to this (e.g., by taking your own food to work).
Craving for certain foods, such as very bland or very spicy food, or foods of a certain texture.	Ensuring that you have a balanced diet with regular check-ups to maintain overall health and watching out for any side-effects such as stomach issues. Consider any potential alternatives that could be healthier, such as replacing soft drinks with fizzy water.
Tendency to chew inedible objects such as clothing or pens.	Chewing gum, working with occupational therapists.
Drooling.	Working with a speech or occupational therapist, changing your sleep position.

Sight (visual system)

Effect	Solution
Over- or undersensitivity to light, possibly causing pain or difficulty sleeping.	Eye masks when sleeping, sunglasses, blackout curtains, adapting environment to suit you, such as having lamps or certain light bulbs.
Difficulty understanding how far an object is away from you in space, causing clumsiness or accidents.	Working with an occupational therapist to develop this awareness and practising training activities, removing dangerous objects from your environment or putting stickers on things such as gates!
Difficulty reading and processing written text, for example, by speed-reading but not taking in any information.	Underlining books as reading, talking about what you are reading with another person, or writing notes on it afterwards. Doing strengthening exercises such as wordsearches.
Difficulty maintaining eye contact.	Reminding yourself to look into a person's eyes when talking to them, imagining a red spot on their forehead.
Messy handwriting or a mix-up of letters and words.	Working with an occupational therapist on this, practising training activities, such as word puzzles or handwriting exercises.

Vestibular system: Our sense of balance and spatial orientation

Effect	Solution
Over-responsive to movement, such as disliking playground swings or fairground rides, lifts or escalators.	Take the stairs! Explaining to others your sensitivities and adapting your environment to adjust.
Motion sickness when travelling.	Avoiding reading or screens whilst travelling, using medication, figuring out which transport works best for you.
Under-responsive to movement, such as being unable to sit still, running instead of walking, moving the body whilst sitting (such as shaking of the legs or tapping of feet).	Using distracting objects, such as beads on a chain, or Rubik's cubes. Taking regular breaks and avoiding extra stimulants such as coffee.
Craving intense, fast experiences, such as fairground rides or spinning on a chair, 'thrill-seeking'.	Engaging in safe and measured activities such as visiting a theme park (or getting a season ticket!), taking up hobbies such as rock-climbing.

cont.

Effect	Solution
Losing balance easily and being clumsy, falling over often or dropping things, difficulties in activities requiring good balance, such as riding a bike.	Taking extra care when doing balance-related activities (such as using bicycle stabilisers!), adapting your environment suitably, such as having a soft carpet to fall onto or a very tough phone case!

Proprioceptive system: How we control our own body and muscles

Effect	Solution
Sensory-seeking behaviour related to the muscles, such as excessive jumping and stomping of feet, swinging legs when sitting at a table, cracking knuckles.	Ensuring you aren't hurting yourself in these activities, avoiding extra stimulants such as caffeine, explaining your sensitivities to the people around you if it is distracting to them.
Seeking 'tight' feelings, such as strong hugs or many blankets at bedtime.	Weighted blankets, deep tissue massages, good hugs!
Misjudging how to use the muscles for certain activities, such as putting arms into sleeves when getting dressed.	Figuring out how this affects you and adapting your routine to suit, for example by allocating more time to getting dressed in the morning.
Difficulty regulating pressure that is exerted, such as pressing too hard on a keyboard when typing, breaking objects or having messy handwriting.	Taking extra care when applying pressure to things and explaining your sensitivities to others or adapting your environment as appropriate, for example by using a Dictaphone instead of taking notes.

Interoception: How we understand our body's inner sensations, such as our internal organs

Effect	Solution
Over- or under-responsiveness to our internal sensations, such as being able to strongly feel (or ignore!) the need to go to the bathroom.	Being compassionate to yourself and adapting your environment appropriately, such as acting as soon as you feel a 'need' in your body and knowing where the bathroom is! Try to develop a routine with 'must-do' activities each day, such as drinking water even though you might not feel thirsty or eating three meals a day.

Being aware of certain sensations others might usually not, such as the feeling of a heart beating.	Assessing how this impacts you and being compassionate to yourself – everyone has the same experiences, some are just more aware than others!
Not being able to feel pain as others might feel it, such as not realising when you have hurt yourself and later finding bruises!	Being extra careful to avoid hurting yourself, such as putting a layer of material on any sharp edges you might be prone to walking into.
Having trouble feeling and identifying emotions, as a result of being out of touch with bodily sensations such as tense muscles and shallow breathing. This could cause a feeling of 'numbness'.	Setting reminders to identify how you are feeling throughout the day. You might just need a few extra seconds to settle into the body and do a scan to understand how you might be feeling at any one time.
Craving interoceptive input and 'feelings' – for example, doing things such as eating excessively fast, gripping of the hands or pinching yourself.	Trying to slow down and be mindful of how 'fast' you are living, and addressing any potentially self-harming habits. Tools such as stress balls could give be a healthier option than gripping your own hands!
Overreacting to sensory feelings, such as eating more when feeling hungry.	Try to sense how you feel when you are feeling 'comfortable' by doing a scan of how all the different parts of your body are feeling. Try to keep this 'normal' benchmark in mind when feeling new sensations such as hunger and eating.

It's really helpful to go through the senses above and write down how you typically experience each one. It can help to make a lot of sense out of childhood habits and things we do without understanding why – try to have compassion for yourself when considering how this has impacted your life.

An important practice for ADHD-ers to do is regularly checking in to your body to understand how you're feeling – not just emotionally, but physically. I can often find myself curled up into very uncomfortable sitting positions for hours on end without realising! Think about setting a reminder to check in to your body and just sense how each part of your body is feeling, as we will discuss in 'Z is for Zen'.

Being aware of this is vital to ensuring that you are living as comfortable and happy a life as possible, and, importantly, communicating this to others. As in 'L is for Love', relationship issues can easily arise through miscommunications related to ADHD, and if you can't understand your own ADHD, then you can't communicate this to others.

is for Zen

Did you know?

- One in three people who have been diagnosed with ADHD have also experienced depression. It is estimated that 18.6 per cent of adults are affected by both ADHD and depression (CHADD, 2019).

- It has been reported that 8.3 per cent of 585 adults with ADHD had a co-morbid mood (9.3%), anxiety (8.8%), substance-use (11.5%) or behavioural (15.6%) disorder (ADHD Institute, 2019).

- Meditation over a long period can result in different patterns in our brain, especially in the frontal region, and increase dopamine levels, which are impacted by ADHD (Sherman, 2022).

If you've made it this far (including skim-reading or skipping chapters) – well done! This chapter is all about mindfulness and mental well-being. People with ADHD are highly likely to experience other mental health conditions, such as anxiety or depression, due to a range of factors, including the impact of having ADHD in a 'non-ADHD' world!

'M is for Medication' provides a helpful overview of treatment for ADHD, but it is a good idea to speak to your doctor about any other possible issues that you might be encountering. It's vital to accept that you are not a superhuman immune to any other mental health conditions because of receiving treatment for ADHD, and not to see this as a weakness. It can feel overwhelming to get to grips with one mental health condition and any more can seem simply terrifying.

Ultimately, none of us have any idea of what we are doing here. We are little bags of jelly held up by bones, and our bodies are working away to keep us alive, largely without us even realising. ADHD is a label that we have apportioned to a certain set of characteristics and neurological make-up, but that doesn't mean that it is 'bad'; it's just how your brain works – which is pretty brilliantly, on the whole!

Mindfulness and self-improvement can become as much as an addiction as any of our other ADHD-fuelled interests. There are certain techniques and practices, however, that can have a hugely beneficial effect on our overall mental well-being, which it's good to bear in mind for times of stress.

Meditation

This is the practice of training our attention and focus, usually associated with concentrating on breathing for a particular length of time. There are many different types of meditating, and, in my experience, the sitting still for long periods of time doesn't work particularly well with ADHD. We already have trouble staying still, quiet and focused in normal life, let alone when we are left to create havoc inside our own minds with a specific goal of *not* thinking. For me, meditation is the process of training my brain to think more slowly and implement the 'thinking time' before making decisions, as discussed in 'T is for Time Management'.

Meditation is the antidote to overthinking and impulsivity, by training our brains to slow down, relax and pause between thoughts. However, if we try to force ourselves to meditate in ways that don't work for us (such as sitting quietly for an hour!), we may end up beating ourselves up and quitting.

To figure out your own way of meditating, think about what makes you feel calm and has the potential to 'turn your brain off'. Any times that you've felt completely at peace with the world, such as after a yoga class or swimming in the ocean. These tend to be activities that make us feel present and 'in the moment', such as exercising, walking or drawing, where thinking has taken a back seat to being – sometimes referred to as a 'state of flow'.

As in 'V is for Vices', ADHD-ers may be prone to developing unhealthy strategies to turn off their brains, so it's important to distinguish between 'good' and 'bad' activities. Drinking alcohol until your mind turns off isn't recommended!

When you have figured out your best fit for meditating, think about how you can incorporate this into your daily life, such as going for a run in the morning. We can sometimes need a bit of help reminding ourselves to relax, so it's good to schedule this into your routine or set yourself visual reminders.

If you prefer to try the form of meditating whilst focusing on your breath, there are good apps such as Calm and Headspace which have a variety of engaging ways to make meditating a little bit easier.

Checking in with ourselves: Body scans

As seen in 'Y is for Your Body', ADHD can have a huge impact on the way we experience the world around us through our senses. We might be more or less aware than neurotypical people would be of things such as background noises, lights, uncomfortable clothing, pain, temperature – the list is endless. Living in a world where we are feeling constantly stimulated can use up a *lot* of mental energy on a subconscious level, and we might not even realise that we are becoming stressed out at something – until it is too late!

It's also useful to check in with ourselves regularly to understand how we are feeling at any one time. For example, we might have needed to go to the bathroom for an hour but ignored this need until we actually 'thought' it, or have not eaten food because we are so hyper-focused that we don't recognise we are actually really hungry. Feelings are what indicate action, and they are there for an important reason! It can sometimes feel difficult to get out of my head and into my body, so these kinds of scans are really useful in connecting the two.

To do a body scan, simply think about each part of your body in turn. You might want to consciously consider the senses, such as asking yourself what you can feel, touch, smell, taste and so on at any one time. Or you might prefer to run through the body from your head to your feet, checking in with each part of yourself to simply 'feel' it. I find it useful to imagine that my body is a giant colouring book, and I am colouring in the parts according to how they're currently feeling. I tend to hold a LOT of tension in my body without realising! It's good to try to consciously 'relax' each part of your body.

These exercises are really useful to do a few times a day, if possible, even as mini 'mind-breaks', so consider setting yourself regular reminders to 'drop in' to your body.

Checking in with ourselves: Feeling our feelings

It's also helpful to assess how we are feeling mentally, by asking ourselves questions such as 'How am I feeling? Am I feeling angry? Sad? Happy? Scared? Angry? Disgusted?'

It can sometimes be really difficult to understand how we are feeling at any one time, so this is good to do in combination with a body scan. The body sends us signals, such as tension to indicate anger or a fast heartbeat if we're feeling scared or the clenching of teeth if we are feeling angry.

By identifying a feeling, we can then feel it. This might be by simply sitting and allowing it to wash over us, such as with a release of crying. Or we might feel in different ways, such as writing out our feelings on paper. It's important that we allow our feelings to properly surface instead of trying to suppress them (even subconsciously!), to make sure that we can properly identify and act upon our needs. Feelings are what is so magic about being human – we are able to experience life in a huge variety of ways, and the negative feelings are as important to allow as the positive ones.

We are often told to just 'cheer up', 'think positively' or consider how lucky we are in comparison to others, as though this would fix our stresses. This usually makes us feel worse for having negative feelings at the same time as trying to get rid of them, when the only way to truly release them is by allowing them to be there. If we ignore our own needs, then we end up people-pleasing, as in 'N is for No', and missing out on a lot of our own life by prioritising others instead.

Try to check in with your feelings at least once a day. We can learn to regulate our feelings in this way, by accepting them instead of trying to ignore them.

Identifying our needs

As a combination of the two previous exercises, it is important to regularly take the time to identify your needs when you have ADHD. If we aren't in touch with our feelings or bodies, and don't take the time to think things out slowly, we may be very prone to ignoring any of our own needs.

For example, think about your response to the question 'How are you?' I automatically say 'I'm good thanks, how are you?' without even considering how I am actually doing. If someone asks me if I need anything, my answer tends to automatically be no, and I have to stop myself with a reminder to actually think about whether I do need something. The real answer is often very different! This relates to people-pleasing, as in 'N is for No', but even with this awareness, it can be difficult to acknowledge our own needs if we have had a lifetime of ignoring them.

Our needs may vary depending on the situation. We might need a change in temperature/clothing if we feel hot or cold, more sleep if we're feeling tired, to go to the bathroom or to get some fresh air. Other needs could be taking a break from work, changing the position we are sitting in, exercise, food, drink, human connection, safety – quite literally anything at all.

Needs are typically defined as things that are necessary for our survival, and this is where we should exercise our prioritising muscles. It can be overwhelming to think of all the things we might need in one situation, and how to distinguish them from things we simply *want*. For example, needing a glass of water versus a glass of wine!

A good rule of thumb is asking yourself: *How could I feel more comfortable in this situation right now?*

Try to identify at least one thing every time you ask yourself the question. There is always likely to be something that you can do to feel more comfortable in any situation, even if it's just taking a deep breath in.

Another way you can check in with your basic needs is to run through some simple questions as a baseline, whenever you notice yourself feeling stressed. These could include:

→ Do I feel safe?

→ When did I last drink water/eat a meal?

→ Am I hot or cold?

→ When did I last shower?

→ When did I last go outside?

→ When did I last exercise?

→ When did I last see or speak to another person?

→ How much sleep did I get last night?

→ How can I help myself right now?

Some people may find that they can identify their needs more easily by writing in a journal, for example, or by speaking out loud. Whatever works best for you, make sure it's a question you're asking yourself often throughout the day and that you are acting upon the answers, communicating this to others where necessary!

Being aware of our inner voice and thoughts

As in 'K is for Kindness', ADHD-ers can often be quite mean to themselves, sometimes without even realising! It's important to regularly tune in to your inner voice to see how you are treating yourself. It might seem silly to do this, but if you sit quietly for a minute, then thoughts are likely to start popping up.

Notice what you are thinking about. Are you berating yourself for not doing enough or being enough? Replaying an embarrassing scenario over in your head? Worrying about whether somebody likes you or not? Worrying about the possible worst-case scenario? Criticising yourself for your looks?

When our radio is set to 'self-compassion' mode, the above types of thoughts won't bother us so much. We might chuckle to ourselves as an embarrassing situation replays, then let it go. We consciously decide not to worry about whether someone likes us or not, because we *like us*, and it doesn't really matter at the end of the day. We accept ourselves, and so these issues don't seem such a big deal.

If you've only ever listened to the 'mean' radio, it's very hard to change stations, but it can be done. The idea is to catch every mean thought and turn it around, to start sticking up for yourself, to yourself. Think of yourself as calling into a radio show to complain about what you're hearing that's inaccurate! You are perfectly great as you are! These radio presenters need firing! One of my most life-changing moments was realising that the thoughts in my head are not me, and that I can actually change them.

This can be done by taking our thoughts and asking ourselves the below questions, which have been adapted from Byron Katie:[1]

1. Is this thought true? (e.g. X doesn't like me – what's the proof for this?)

2. Can I say with absolute certainty that it is true? (e.g. No, I cannot say for sure, because I am not in X's head)

3. How do I react when I believe this thought? (e.g. become upset, frustrated, self-sabotage, dislike X)

4. Who would I be without the thought? (e.g. calm, happy, not upset with X)

5. What's the opposite of the thought? (e.g. X likes me!)

By doing this, we can see that most of what we are telling ourselves are *stories*. Choose to tell yourself the story that makes you feel best.

This applies for all your life. ADHD can either be your favourite part of yourself or something you try to resist. I really hope that this book has helped you realise how having ADHD is a superpower and something to be celebrated – you are something to be celebrated. Now that you have an understanding of the way your brain works, you can do anything you put your mind to. Good luck!

---

1   https://thework.com

References

Adamou, M., Arif, M., Asherson, P. *et al.* (2013) 'Occupational issues of adults with ADHD.' *BMC Psychiatry 13,* 59. Retrieved on May 13, 2022 from https://bmcpsychiatry.biomedcentral.com: https://bmcpsychiatry.biomedcentral.com/articles/10.1186/1471-244X-13-59.

ADDitude (2020) 'Great job! A career happiness formula for adults with ADHD.' Retrieved on June 12, 2020 from www.additudemag.com/best-jobs-adhd-careers.

ADHD Australia (2019) 'The role of Executive Functions.' Retrieved on May 5, 2022 from www.adhdaustralia.org.au/about-adhd/the-role-of-executive-functioning-in-adhd.

ADHD Awareness Month (2020) 'Seven facts about ADHD.' Retrieved on May 13, 2022 from https://adhdawarenessmonth.org/myths-vs-facts.

ADHD Foundation (n.d.) Umbrella Project 2021. Retrieved from www.adhdfoundation.org.uk/wp-content/uploads/2020/10/Neurodiversity-Umbrella-Project-2021-2023-Information-for-Businesses-Schools-and-Sponsors-Final-Oct-2020.pdf.

ADHD Institute (2019) 'Comorbidities.' ADHD Institute. Retrieved on May 16, 2022 from https://adhd-institute.com/burden-of-adhd/comorbidities.

American Psychological Association (APA) (2012) 'Girls with ADHD at risk for self-injury, suicide attempts as young adults.' Retrieved on May 13, 2022 from www.apa.org/news/press/releases/2012/08/girls-adhd.

Attention UK (n.d.) 'University support for students with ADHD.' Retrieved on June 12, 2020 from www.attentionuk.org/about/the-state-of-current-provision/university-support-for-students-with-adhd.

Barkley, R. (1988) *Attention Deficit Hyperactive Disorder: A Handbook for Diagnosis and Treatment.* New York: Guilford Press.

Barkley, R. (2011) 'The important role of executive functioning and self-regulation in ADHD.' Retrieved on May 05, 2022 from www.russellbarkley.org/factsheets/ADHD_EF_and_SR.pdf.

Barkley, R (2017) *Barkley: ADHD is Time Blindess.* Retrieved on May 13, 2022 from www.youtube.com/watch?v=fVqFElTrgLw.

BBC News (2018) 'ADHD diagnosis for adults "can take seven years".' Retrieved on June 06, 2022 from www.bbc.co.uk/news/uk-england-44956540.

Becker, S.P. & Lienesch, J.A. (2018) 'Night-time media use in adolescents with ADHD: Links to sleep problems and internalizing symptoms.' *Sleep Medicine 51,* 171–178. Retrieved on May 13, 2022 from https://pubmed.ncbi.nlm.nih.gov/30223187.

Bernstein, J. (2010) 'ADHD and "Honest Lies".' Retrieved on May 13, 2022 from www.psychologytoday.com/gb/blog/liking-the-child-you-love/201002/adhd-and-honest-lies-0.

Bhandari, S. (2o2o) 'What is Rejection Sensitive Dysphoria?' Retrieved from https://www.webmd.com/add-adhd/rejection-sensitive-dysphoria.

Born to Be ADHD (2o17) 'A Lifetime Lost or a Lifetime Saved.' Retrieved on May 13, 2o22 from www.adhdfoundation.org.uk/wp-content/uploads/2o17/11/A-Lifetime-Lost-or-a-Lifetime-Saved-report.pdf.

Breslau, J., Miller, E., W-J.J.Chung & Schweitzer, J.B. (2o11) 'Childhood and adolescent onset psychiatric disorders, substance use, and failure to graduate high school on time.' *Journal of Psychiatric Research 45*, 3, 295–301.

Brody, B. (2o15) 'How common is ADHD?' *WebMD*. Retrieved on May 03, 2o22 from www.webmd.com/add-adhd/guide/adhd-how-common.

Brown, C. & Dunn, W. (2oo2) *Adult/Adolescent Sensory Profile: User's Manual.* San Antonio, TX: The Psychological Corporation.

Campbell, D. 'One in four UK prisoners has attention deficit hyperactivity disorder, says report.' *The Guardian*. Retrieved on August 8, 2o22 from www.theguardian.com/society/2o22/jun/18/uk-prisoners-attention-deficit-disorder-adhd-prison.

CHADD (2o17) 'Hormones and women's ADHD symptoms – Part Two.' *ADHD Weekly*, 10 August. Retrieved on May 12, 2o22 from https://chadd.org/adhd-weekly/hormones-and-womens-adhd-symptoms-part-two.

CHADD (2o19) 'When depression co-occurs with ADHD.' *ADHD Weekly,* July 19. Retrieved on May 13, 2o22 from https://chadd.org/adhd-weekly/when-depression-co-occurs-with-adhd.

Cherney, K. (2o19) 'ADHD and brain structure and function.' Retrieved November 28, 2o2o, from www.healthline.com/health/adhd/the-brains-structure-and-function#brain-structure-and-function.

Chesapeake Center, The (n.d.) 'Life management tools for women with ADHD.' Retrieved on May 12, 2o2o from https://chesapeakeadd.com/home/education-and-training/articles/life-management-tools-for-women-with-adhd.

Comres (2o17) 'Shire ADHD at school survey.' Retrieved on June o6, 2o22 from comresglobal.com/polls/shire-adhd-at-school-survey.

Conjero, I. *et al.* (2o19) 'Association of symptoms of attention deficit-hyperactivity disorder and impulsive-aggression with severity of suicidal behavior in adult attempters.' *Scientific Reports 9*, Retrieved on May 13, 2o22 from www.nature.com/articles/s41598-019-41046-y.

Cook, J. *et al.* (2o14) 'The self-esteem of adults diagnosed with attention-deficit/hyperactivity disorder (ADHD): A systematic review of the literature.' *ADHD Attention Deficit Hyperactivity Disorders 6*, 249–268. Retrieved on May 15, 2o22 from https://link.springer.com/article/10.1007/s12402-014-0133-2.

Csikszentmihalyi, M. & Csikszentmihalyi, I.S. (1988) *Optimal Experience: Psychological Studies of Flow in Consciousness.* Cambridge: Cambridge University Press.

Deschanel, Z. (2o11) 'Crafternoon with Zooey D.' Retrieved on June o6, 2o22 from http://web.archive.org/web/2o15o123o8o6o6/http:/hellogiggles.com/crafternoon-with-zooey-d.

Dodson, W. (2o16) 'Emotional regulation and rejection sensitivity.' Retrieved on May 15, 2o22 from https://chadd.org/wp-content/uploads/2o16/10/ATTN_10_16_EmotionalRegulation.pdf.

Dodson, W. (2o22) 'ADHD and sleep problems: This is why you're always so tired.' *ADDitude*. Retrieved on June o6, 2o22 from www.additudemag.com/adhd-sleep-disturbances-symptoms.

Driver and Vehicle Licensing Agency (2o2o) 'Psychiatric disorders: Assessing fitness to drive.' Retrieved June 12, 2o2o from www.gov.uk/guidance/psychiatric-disorders-assessing-fitness-to-drive#pervasive-developmental-disorders-and-adhd.

Equality Act (2o1o) www.legislation.gov.uk/ukpga/2o1o/15/contents?msclkid=67430dd7bo2711ec99e4b329ea1ad83b.

Fuller-Thompson, E. *et al.* (2o2o) 'The dark side of ADHD: Factors associated with suicide attempts among those with

ADHD in a national representative Canadian sample.' *Archives of Suicide Research*, December. Retrieved on May 12, 2022 from www.tandfonline.com/doi/full/10.1080/13811118.2020.1856258?scroll=top&needAccess=true.

Haupt, A. (2010) 'Can your relationship survive ADHD?' *USNews,* September 28. Retrieved on May 15, 2022 from https://health.usnews.com/health-news/family-health/brain-and-behavior/articles/2010/09/28/can-your-relationship-survive-adhd.

Hillman, C.H. *et al.* (2019) 'Effects of the FITKids Randomized Controlled Trial on executive control and brain function.' *Pediatrics 134,* 4. Retrieved on May 16, 2022 from https://pediatrics.aappublications.org/content/134/4/e1063.

Holland, K. & Riley, E. (2014) 'ADHD numbers: Facts, statistics, and you.' Retrieved on May 15, 2022 from www.addrc.org/adhd-numbers-facts-statistics-and-you.

Hupfeld, K.E., Abagis, T.R. & Shah, P. (2019) 'Living "in the zone": Hyperfocus in adult ADHD.' *ADHD Attention Deficit and Hyperactivity Disorders 11,* 191–208. Retrieved on May 15, 2022 from https://link.springer.com/article/10.1007/s12402-018-0272-y.

Jellinek, M.S. (2010) 'Don't let ADHD crush children's self esteem.' WebMDedge. Retrieved on June 06, 2022 from www.mdedge.com/psychiatry/article/23971/pediatrics/dont-let-adhd-crush-childrens-self-esteem.

Jones, R. (2022) '"Shopping is a nightmare": how ADHD affects people's spending habits.' *The Guardian.* Retrieved on August 8, 2022 from www.theguardian.com/money/2022/jun/25/shopping-adhd-spending-habits.

Karolinska Institutet (2012) 'ADHD treatment "may reduce risk of criminal behaviour".' *New England Journal of Medicine,* November 22.

Kuriyan, A.B. *et al.* (2013) 'ADHD and long-term outcomes.' *Journal of Abnormal Child Psychology 41,* 1, 27–41.

LancUK (2012) 'ADHD and Crime.' Retrieved on May 15, 2022 from www.lanc.org.uk/adhd-and-crime.

LancUK (2016) 'Our history.' Retrieved on November 28, 2020 from www.lanc.org.uk/about-us-adhd-asd-assessment/our-history.

Liao, C. (2020) 'ADHD Symptoms and Financial Distress.' *Review of Finance 25,* 4. Retrieved on May 15, 2020 from https://academic.oup.com/rof/article/25/4/1129/5824803.

Lindsay, M. (2020) 'ADHD assessment system "broken" with five-year waiting times.' *BBC,* 28 July. Retrieved on May 13, 2022 from www.bbc.co.uk/news/uk-england-53526174.

LoPorto, G. (2005) The Da Vinci Method. Concord, MA: Media for Your Mind, Inc.

Maskell, L. (2022) *The Reality Manifesto.* Self-published. Available from www.amazon.co.uk/Reality-Manifesto-Z-anti-exploitation-manual/dp/B09XSX7YGN.

May, R. (2019) 'Start ups across the UK are going bust – they need more careful management for our economy to boom.' *The Telegraph,* January 24. Retrieved from www.telegraph.co.uk/politics/2019/01/24/start-ups-across-uk-going-bust-need-careful-management-economy.

Mazzone, L. *et al.* (2013) 'Self-Esteem Evaluation in Children and Adolescents Suffering from ADHD.' *Clinical Practice & Epidemiology in Mental Health 9,* 96–102. Retrieved on May 15, 2022 from www.ncbi.nlm.nih.gov/pmc/articles/PMC3715757.

Meijer, S. (2019) 'ADHD can make it harder to manage your money. Here's some tips to help.' Retrieved on May 15, 2022 from www.abc.net.au/news/2019-05-31/how-adhd-affects-your-wallet-mental-health-kids/11158952.

Miranda, M.C. *et al.* (2012) 'Performance patterns in Conners' CPT among children with attention deficit hyperactivity disorder and dyslexia.' *Arquivos de Neuro-Psiquiatria 70,* 2, 91–96.

Mitchell, J.T. *et al.* (2017) 'A pilot trial of mindfulness meditation training for ADHD in adulthood: Impact on core symptoms, executive functioning, and emotion dysregulation.' *Journal of Attention Disorders 21, 13, 1105–1120.*

Moya, J. et al. (2014) 'The impact of persisting hyperactivity on social relationships.' Journal of Attention Disorders 18, 1, 52–60. Retrieved on May 16, 2022 from www.ncbi.nlm.nih.gov/pmc/articles/PMC3867339.

National Collaborating Centre for Mental Health (2009) 'Attention Deficit Hyperactivity Disorder: The NICE guideline on diagnosis and management of ADHD in children, young people and adults.' The British Psychological Society and the Royal College of Psychiatrists.

National Institute for Health and Care Excellence (2019) Attention deficit hyperactivity disorder: diagnosis and management. NICE Guideline [NG87]. Retrieved on June 12, 2020 from www.nice.org.uk/guidance/ng87/resources/attention-deficit-hyperactivity-disorder-diagnosis-and-management-pdf-1837699732933.

Nigg, J. (2020) 'ADHD, anger, and emotional regulation.' Psychology Today, August 4. Retrieved on May 16, 2020 from www.psychologytoday.com/gb/blog/helping-kids-through-adhd/202008/adhd-anger-and-emotional-regulation.

Office of National Statistics (2020) Divorces in England and Wales. Retrieved on May 16, 2022 from www.ons.gov.uk/peoplepopulationandcommunity/births deaths and marriages/divorce/bulletins/divorcesinenglandandwales/2019.

Olivardia, R. (2018) 'ADHD and obesity: An under-recognized problem.' Attention, October. Retrieved on May 10, 2022 from www.chadd.org/attention-article/adhd-obesity-an-under-recognized-problem.

Oosterloo, M. et al. (2006) 'Possible confusion between primary hypersomnia and adult attention-deficit/hyperactivity disorder.' Psychiatry Research 143, 2–3, 293–297. Retrieved on May 15, 2022 from https://pubmed.ncbi.nlm.nih.gov/16854470.

Palmini, A. (2008) 'Professionally successful adults with attention-deficit/hyperactivity disorder (ADHD): Compensation strategies and subjective effects of pharmacological treatment.' Dementia &

Neuropsychologia 2, 1, 63–70. Retrieved on May 16, 2022 from www.ncbi.nlm.nih.gov/pmc/articles/PMC5619157.

Pera, G. (2015) 'Research: ADHD, balance, and "postural sway".' Retrieved on May 16, 2022 from https://adhdrollercoaster.org/adhd-news-and-research/research-adhd-balance-and-postural-sway.

Perroud, N. et al. (2016) 'Personality profiles in adults with attention deficit hyperactivity disorder (ADHD).' BMC Psychiatry 16, 199. Retrieved on May 16, 2022 from https://bmcpsychiatry.biomedcentral.com/articles/10.1186/s12888-016-0906-6.

Ptacek, R. et al. (2019) 'Clinical implications of the perception of time in Attention Deficit Hyperactivity Disorder (ADHD): A review.' Medical Science Monitor 25, 3918–3924.Retrieved on May 16, 2022 from www.ncbi.nlm.nih.gov/pmc/articles/PMC6556068.

Pychyl, T. (2018) 'ADHD and procrastination' Psychology Today, September 6. Retrieved on May 16, 2022 from www.psychologytoday.com/gb/blog/dont-delay/201809/adhd-and-procrastination.

Ratcliffe, M. (2022) 'Women and girls face ADHD misdiagnosis due to misconceptions around symptoms.' Sky News, 8 January. Retrieved on May 12, 2022 from https://news.sky.com/story/women-and-girls-face-adhd-misdiagnosis-due-to-misconceptions-around-symptoms-12511672.

Robinson, B.E. Chained to the Desk: A Guidebook for Workaholics, Their Partners and Children, and the Clinicians Who Treat Them. New York: NYU Press.

Rodden, J. & Nigg, J. (2020) 'Impulsivity and the ADHD brain: Neural networks explained.' ADDitude. Retrieved on June 06, 2022 from www.additudemag.com/adhd-brain-impulsivity-explained.

Ross, E. (2016) 'This is what it feels like to live with ADHD.' Evening Standard, June 16. Retrieved November 28, 2020 from www.standard.co.uk/lifestyle/this-is-what-it-feels-like-to-live-with-adhd-a3273796.html

Saline, S. (2019) 'How does an ADHD

diagnosis affect self-esteem?' *CHADD, ADHD Weekly,* August 8. Retrieved on May 16, 2022 from www.chadd.org/adhd-weekly/how-does-an-adhd-diagnosis-affect-self-esteem.

Sedgwick, J.A. *et al.* (2018) 'The positive aspects of attention deficit hyperactivity disorder: A qualitative investigation of successful adults with ADHD.' *ADHD Attention Deficit and Hyperactivity Disorders* 11, 241–253. Springer Link. Retrieved on June 12, 2020 from https://link.springer.com/article/10.1007/s12402-018-0277-6.

Sherman, C. (2022) 'Mindfulness meditation: ADHD symptom relief with breath.' ADDitude. Retrieved on June 06, 2022 from www.additudemag.com/mindfulness-meditation-for-adhd.

Shi, Y. et al. (2021) 'Racial disparities in diagnosis of Attention-Deficit/Hyperactivity Disorder in a US national birth cohort.' *JAMA Network Open* 4, 3, e210321. Retrieved May 04, 2022 from https://jamanetwork.com/journals/jamanetworkopen/fullarticle/2776807.

Solis, B. (2019) 'Our digital malaise: Distraction is costing us more than we think.' *LSE Business Review,* 19 April. Retrieved on March 17, 2022 from https://blogs.lse.ac.uk/businessreview/2019/04/19/our-digital-malaise-distraction-is-costing-us-more-than-we-think.

Spencer, T., Biederman, J., Wilens, T. *et al.* (2005) 'A large, double-blind, randomized clinical trial of methylphenidate in the treatment of adults with attention-deficit/hyperactivity disorder.' Biological Psychiatry 57, 5, 456–463.

University of Illinois at Urbana-Champaign (2011) 'Brief diversions vastly improve focus.' *Science Daily,* February 8. Retrieved on May 17, 2022 from www.sciencedaily.com/releases/2011/02/110208131529.htm.

University of Toronto (2020) 'One in four women with ADHD has attempted suicide.' News release, December 22. Retrieved on June 01, 2022 from www.eurekalert.org/news-releases/616886.

Urian, B. (2022) 'Ads Linking ADHD and obesity pulled from Instagram and Tik-Tok. Cerebral Chief Medical Officer says he didn't approve.' *Times,* 27 January. Retrieved on March 17, 2022 from www.techtimes.com/articles/271125/20220127/ads-linking-adhd-and-obesity-pulled-from-instagram-and-tiktok-cerebral-chief-medical-officer-says-he-didnt-approve.htm.

Vanbuskirk, S. (2018) 'When ADHD is all in the family.' Retrieved on November 28, 2020, from www.additudemag.com/is-adhd-hereditary-blog.

Verheul, I. *et al.* (2016) 'The association between attention-deficit/hyperactivity (ADHD) symptoms and self-employment.' *European Journal of Epidemiology 31,* 8, 793–801. Retrieved on May 17, 2020 from www.ncbi.nlm.nih.gov/pmc/articles/PMC5005387.

Watson, S. (2020) 'ADHD and substance abuse.' Retrieved June 12, 2020 from www.webmd.com/add-adhd/adhd-and-substance-abuse-is-there-a-link.

Weiss, M.D. & McBride, N.M. (2018) 'ADHD: A 24-hour disorder.' *Psychiatric Times* 35, 10. Retrieved on May 16, 2020 from www.psychiatrictimes.com/view/adhd-24-hour-disorder.

White, H.A. & Shah, P. (2006) 'Ininhibited imaginations: Creativity in adults with attention-deficit/hyperactivity disorder.' *Personality and Individual Differences* 40, 1121–1131.

White, H.A. & Shah, P. (2011) 'Creative style and achievement in adults with attention-deficit/hyperactivity disorder.' *Science Direct 50,* 5, 673–677.

Wiklund, J., Patzelt, H. & Dimov, D. (2016) 'Entrepreneurship and psychological disorders: How ADHD can be productively harnessed.' *Journal of Business Venturing Insights 6,* 14–20. Retrieved on May 16, 2022 from www.researchgate.net/publication/305769751_Entrepreneurship_and_psychological_disorders_How_ADHD_can_be_productively_harnessed.

Zuss, M. (2012) *The Practice of Theoretical Curiosity.* Brooklyn, NY: Springer.